A JOURNAL OF ORTHODOX FAITH AND CULTURE

ROAD TO EMMAUS

– No. 70-71 –

TROPARION TO THE SAINTS OF SWITZERLAND

As lovely fruit of your saving seed, O Lord
Helvetia offers you the multitude of her saints,
who have grown forth from her soil.
May you guard your church in our lands in deep peace
through their prayers and the power of thy cross,
O gracious All-Merciful One!

SUBSCRIPTIONS AND CORRESPONDENCE
Road to Emmaus, P.O. Box 16021, Portland, OR 97292-0021

Call toll-free (USA): 1-866-783-6628
Monday-Friday 9:00 am to 5:00 pm (Pacific Standard Time, USA)
Email: emmausjournal@juno.com
Web: www.roadtoemmaus.net

Published Quarterly
$30/year, $55/ 2 year, single issue $11.95. (US check or money order or by credit card on our website)

INTERNATIONAL SUBSCRIPTIONS
Canada add $10/year for shipping. Outside North America add $20/year shipping.
Please subscribe by credit card on our website: www.roadtoemmaus.net
or write us at emmausjournal@juno.com

EDITORIAL OFFICES
Valaam Society of America Russian Mission, #10 Bolshaya Pereyaslavskaya, kv. 124, Moscow, Russia 129110

PUBLISHER
Road to Emmaus Foundation, PO Box 198, Maysville, MO 64469
Views expressed in Road to Emmaus are those of the authors and interviewees
featured here, and do not necessarily reflect opinions of the staff or the publisher.

This periodical is indexed in the *ATLA Religion Database*®, a product of the
American Theological Library Association, 300 S. Wacker Dr., Suite 2100, Chicago, IL 60606
Email: atla@atla.com Web: www.atla.com

ISBN: 978-1-63551-069-0

Printed in USA.

Front cover: Saint Beatus Caves near Lake Thun, Switzerland.

Inside front cover: Icon of All Saints of Switzerland. Photo courtesy Bishop Amvrosii (Cantecuzene).

Inside back cover: Abbey of St. Maurice, Saint-Maurice, Switzerland.

With thanks to Mat. Margaret Bauman and Cornelia Delkekamp-Hayes for the use of their pilgrimage photos in this issue.

A JOURNAL OF ORTHODOX FAITH AND CULTURE

ROAD TO EMMAUS

Vol. XVIII, No. 3-4 Summer/Fall 2017 (#70-71)

CONTENTS

EARLY CHRISTIAN PILGRIMAGE SITES OF SWITZERLAND

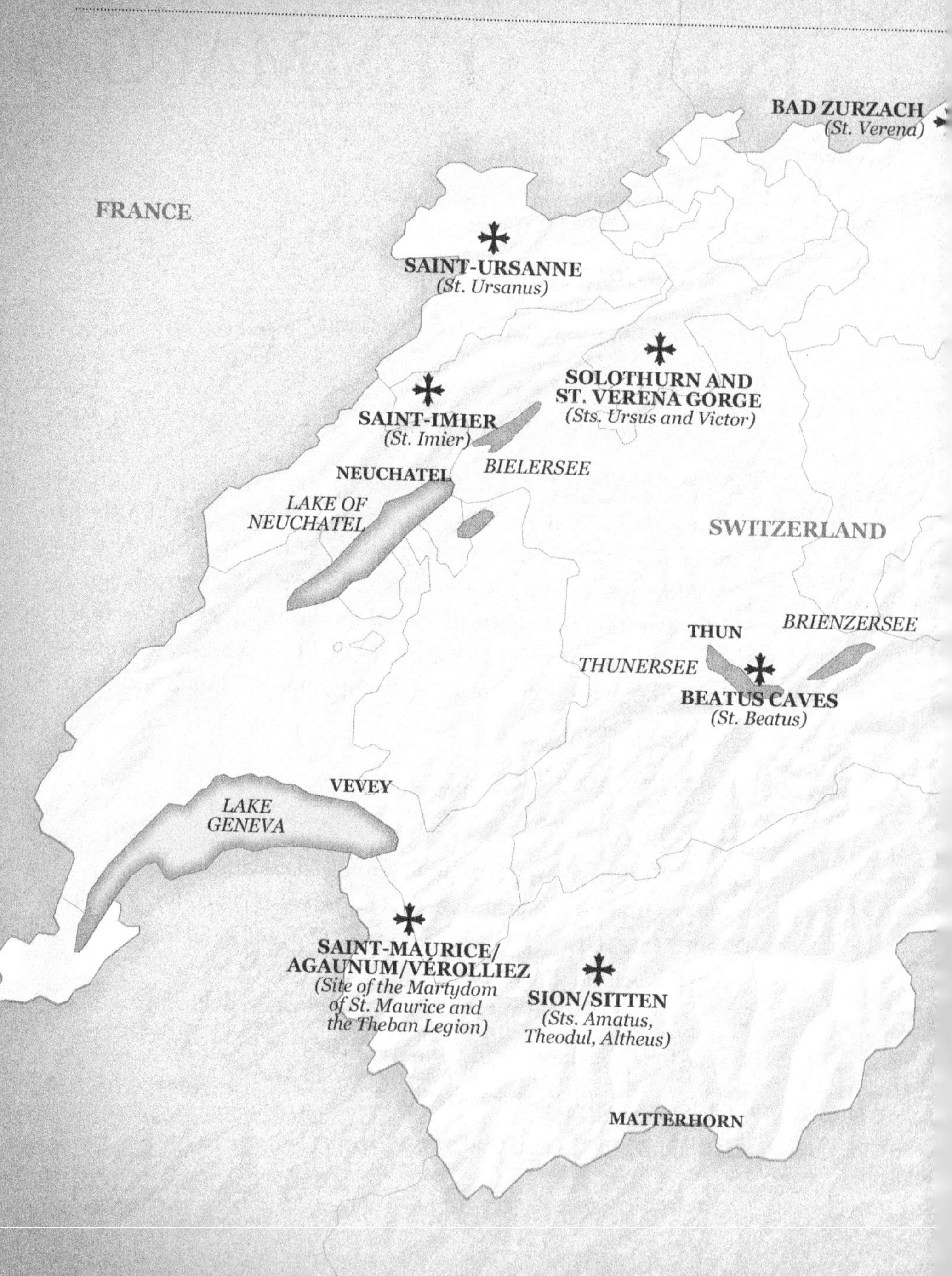

GERMANY

LAKE CONSTANCE

ST. GALLEN
(St. Gall and St. Otmar)

ZURICH

ZURICHSEE

LIECHTENSTEIN

AUSTRIA

ZUGERSEE

WALENSEE

EINSIEDELN
(St. Meinrad)

LAKE OF LUCERNE

CHUR
(Sts. Asinio, Lucius, and Valentian)

DISENTIS
(St. Sigisbert)

CAZIS/TOMILS
(St. Victor of Tomils and Cazis)

ANDERMATT
(Sts. Felix, Regula, and Exuperantius)

LAKE COMO

AKE MAGGIORE

LAKE OF LUGANO

Our Guest Authors and Pilgrims

Road to Emmaus Journal is pleased to introduce our guest pilgrims and authors for this issue on the saints and holy places of Switzerland: Popadia Margaret Bauman and Cornelia Delkeskamp-Hayes, whose long friendship and interest in Orthodoxy in German-speaking lands have inspired their pilgrimages to many early Christian sites.

Popadia Margaret Bauman of the Joy of All Who Sorrow Bulgarian Orthodox Church in Indianapolis, Indiana, of German and Swiss parentage and a teacher of German, has spent almost two decades preparing material for her forthcoming Orthodox guide to pre-schism Christian sites in Germany, Austria, Switzerland, and small areas of France, Italy and Luxembourg. From the early 1960's to 1979, she spent seven years living in Munich, Cologne, and Amsterdam, first as a student and then as a Christian missionary. In 2001, Pda. Margaret made her first trip back to Germany and Switzerland as an Orthodox Christian, and later visited sites in Holland, Belgium, Germany and Austria. This is her second issue with *Road to Emmaus Journal*; in 2010 she researched and authored two articles for Issue #41: "Orthodox Roots, Woods, and Water: A Decade of Pilgrimage to Germany and Switzerland" and "The Advent of Orthodoxy in the German-Speaking Lands."

Raised as a German Protestant, Corinna (Cornelia) Delkeskamp-Hayes grew up and studied mostly in Bonn, and later taught as an Assistant Professor of Philosophy at Pennsylvania State University before moving back to Germany to start a family with her husband Michael. Baptized in the Serbian Church in 1998 on the day of St. Kornelius of Komel, Cornelia presently works as a private scholar, presenting papers in Europe, the U.S., and China. She also serves as editor of *Christian Bioethics: Non-Ecumenical Studies in Medical Morality* and on the editorial board of *The Journal of Medicine and Philosophy*. This is Cornelia's second issue with us, as she also contributed an interview to Issue #41: "Coming Into One's Own Among Strangers at Home," an interview on Orthodoxy and the Christian climate in contemporary Germany.

Opposite: Cornelia Delkeskamp-Hayes and Pda. Margaret Bauman.

Ruins of ancient Roman road in Valais, Switzerland.

I
CHRISTIANITY COMES OVER THE ALPS

A SHORT HISTORY OF EARLY CHRISTIANITY IN SWITZERLAND

An Orthodox convert of German-Swiss heritage, Popadia Margaret Bauman speaks with *Road to Emmaus* about Switzerland's early Christian history.

ROAD TO EMMAUS: Popadia Margaret, can you give us an overview of the conversion of Switzerland to Christianity?

PDA. MARGARET: We know that after the prehistoric period, parts of Switzerland and western Europe were occupied by Celtic peoples, and in 15 BC this territory became part of the Roman Empire after a massive military campaign that entered the region over the Alpine passes from Italy. After arriving on the Swiss Plateau, the Romans continued northward, conquering territory to the Danube, including most of present-day Switzerland and into Germany.[1]

As everywhere, the Romans built their famous roads, towns, and military outposts, as well as bringing in army veterans as settlers, which made it easier for merchants and civil officials to follow them into new areas. Settlements and forts were built along rivers, lakes, and transit roads that crossed the great passes over the Alps into Switzerland.

1 Ed. Note: At the time of Christ, the territory of modern-day Switzerland was divided between the Roman provinces of Raetia et Vindelicia, Gallia Belgica, and at one point the province of Upper Germania. but as with all Roman provinces, boundaries changed over time and Diocletian's reforms in the third century divided the Swiss territory between five different provinces. These amalgamated over hundreds of years, but Switzerland as we know it today only came into being in the early 19th century.

Opposite: Roman theatre ruins, Kaiser-Augst, Switzerland.

As active Roman defense was mostly along the northern borders, the 150 years after Rome's conquest were relatively peaceful for the Swiss territories. The Roman and Celtic populations intermarried, and Rome's more sophisticated administrative structure and laws, agriculture and water systems, architecture, art, and literature took hold – mostly in the cities, although there were also large country villas engaged in agriculture and viniculture.

From the Time of the Apostles to the Early Fourth Century

Christianity began to spread soon after Pentecost and Christians also came to the area we now call Switzerland. There is little factual information about Christians in Switzerland in the first centuries, but traditions were passed down and we can make educated guesses from what was happening in adjacent parts of the empire. For example, St. Polycarp, Bishop of Smyrna (70-155), and disciple of St. John the Theologian, had this to say:

> And although there are different languages throughout the world, yet the content of what has been passed down is one and the same. For the churches which were founded in Germania do not believe or pass on anything different from the ones in Spain or the Celts, those in the Orient or those in Egypt, those in Libya or in the middle of the world. Just as God's sun is one and the same throughout the whole world, so does the news of the Truth penetrate everywhere and enlightens all people who desire to come to the Truth.

By "Germania" (plural in the original text) both "Germania inferior" and "Germania superior" are meant. Upper Germania includes those who inhabited the Jura and the Middle Land in western and central Switzerland.[2] Another early report of Christianity in Switzerland is found in St. Irenaeus' work, *Against Heresies*, written in 180.

We also have evidence from the nearby city of Lyon in Gaul (present-day France), at the confluence of the Rhône and Saône Rivers, which was a great pagan religious site, and later a center of Christianity. It was inhabited by a variety of peoples including Greek and Middle Eastern Christians, as well as

2 Steudler, Andreas, *Aus den Anfängen des Christentums in der Schweiz*, self-published, Bern, 1994, p. 9.

Opposite: Sts. Exuperantus, Felix, and Regula, martyred in Zürich.

Gallo-Romans. Lyon's Christians underwent a fierce persecution in the year 177, when many were martyred under Marcus Aurelius. Among them was St. Pothinus, first bishop of Lyon, sent to Gaul by St. Polycarp around 150.

We know about these remarkable events because of a letter sent to the Christians of what was then called Asia and Phrygia, describing what happened. It is extraordinary that this letter has been preserved, and without it we would know little of early Christianity in Gaul. It is quite probable that Christian activity also existed in the more established Roman settlements of what is now Switzerland, including missionary activity and martyrdom. There were certainly many Greek merchants traveling through, as well as soldiers from Rome and other parts of the empire who may have come from Christian families or been converts themselves. Who knows what other documents or artifacts may eventually turn up?

There are also legends, written down centuries later, concerning the early apostolic period in Switzerland: one tells of a St. Lucius who baptized people at the time of the Apostle Paul; another concerns St. Beatus, who was purportedly baptized in Britain by St. Barnabas and ordained in Rome by St. Peter. He was then sent to Switzerland with a companion named Achates and became a successful missionary in the Aargau and Thurgau regions, finally retiring to a hermitage in a cave above Lake Thun.

These traditions of Lucius and Beatus are complicated by the likelihood that their stories got mixed with the lives of later saints. Still, it is interesting that the belief in apostolic missionary work lingers in post-Reformation Switzerland, and we cannot rule out a core of truth in these stories or the role they played in strengthening the faith of the early Christians.

We also know of the continuous veneration of other early saints who played an important role in the spread of Christianity in the Swiss territories. First the martyrs of the Theban Legion, including: St. Maurice and the legionnaires in Agaunum (now the town of St. Maurice); Sts. Felix and Regula, with their servant Exuperantius in Zürich; Sts. Urs and Victor in Solothurn; as well as the Egyptian hermitess and healer St. Verena who was associated with the Theban Legion, but escaped martyrdom. All of these are said to have lived around the year 300, and the sites of their martyrdoms and St. Verena's ministry became important pilgrimage destinations.

Opposite: Romanesque crypt under Cathedral of St. Pierre, Geneva.

After the Persecutions: Fourth-Century Christianity

From the second century, Christians worshipped secretly in families or small groups during periods of persecution, until they were guaranteed freedom of worship and restoration of property under the Edict of Milan of 313, an agreement between Emperors Constantine and Licinius. Emperor Constantine's conversion and support of Christianity was another impetus to growth, and soon we start seeing churches and baptisteries, even within Roman fortresses. Archeologists have found such traces in Geneva, Kaiseraugst, Zurzach, Martigny, and other places in Switzerland. In the fourth century, we also begin seeing Christian gravestones and objects with Christian symbols (mostly fish, anchors, or the Chi-Rho), and records of the first bishops, such as the signature of St. Theodor of Martigny at a synod in Aquileia (Byzantine Italy) in 381.

I have seen some of these early artifacts in the State Museum in Zürich and in the Roman Museum in Augst (outside of Basel), where there are also excavations of an old baptistery in a cave on a riverbank. They all attest to the presence of Christianity in the Roman settlements of fourth-century Switzerland, particularly a red sandstone grave marker from 350, the oldest known witness to Christianity in Switzerland. Headed by an inscribed anchor, a typical Christian grave symbol, the Latin text follows:

> To the Manes and the eternal
> memory of Eustata, the
> much-loved wife, who lived
> for 65 years. Amatus (her husband)
> has placed this stone.[3]

These historical finds also help us to locate individual Christian parishes, which would have followed the routes of Rome's territorial gains. In the eastern part of present-day Switzerland, Roman roads led over the Raetian passes to Chur; and in the West, over the Great St. Bernard Pass to Martigny

3 Ed. note: "Manes" refers to the spirits and souls of one's ancestors, while the anchor is undoubtedly a Christian symbol. In these early centuries, Christian belief and pagan custom sometimes existed side by side, but if "manes" here is in fact a memorial to family forebearers, it would not necessarily have been in conflict with Christian belief.

and up the Rhône River to Geneva. Radiating from these points, a circle of cities with Christian traces can be drawn along the Rhine border from Chur to Arbon, Stein am Rhein, Zurzach, Kaiseraugst and Basel, and coming from western Switzerland through Lausanne, Yverdon, Avenches, Solothurn, Olten, Windisch and Zürich.

According to Bonjour et al., in *A Short History of Switzerland*[4]: "By the end of the fourth century we may assume a thin network of Christian churches over western Switzerland, with bishops at Lyon, Avenches, Basel, Martigny and Geneva." It is likely that the sparse Celto-Roman population in isolated areas still sacrificed to the old gods.

The growth of Christianity continued under the Romans who made Christianity the state religion in 380, but this was only a few decades before Roman troops withdrew to protect Italy, leaving Switzerland to the incoming Germanic tribes.

The Germanic Invasions

RTE: Who ruled these territories after the Romans, and how did new rulers affect the spread of Christianity?

PDA. MARGARET: Let me just point out that even though I say Switzerland, under Roman rule, today's Swiss regions were part of provinces which also included territories of present-day France, Italy, Germany or Austria. These divisions sometimes corresponded to language differences, and to how quickly Christianity was being assimilated.

Secondly, most of the so-called "barbarian tribes" that later ruled parts of Switzerland were not totally alien to Roman culture or even to Christianity. Some of them had lived in border areas where they not only traded with Romans, but observed and even imitated Roman practices. Great numbers also served in the Roman armies. Before the Romans left, groups of Burgundians had already been allowed to settle in Switzerland with their capital in Geneva. Later, they spread northwest through what are now the French-speaking areas of Switzerland. The Burgundians initially followed the Arian heresy, but in time became Christian and supported the growth of the Church. In 534 they were conquered and annexed by the Franks, who had only been Christian for a generation, since the conversion of King Clovis

4 E. Bonjour, H.S. Offler, and G.R. Potter, *A Short History of Switzerland*, Clarendon Press, Oxford, 1952.

in 496. Conversion to Christianity in the west of Switzerland seems to have occurred between 350 and 700.

Christianity did not spread as quickly or smoothly to the eastern regions of Switzerland, arriving there about 200-300 years later. The Roman influence was weaker here and fewer Celto-Roman Christian outposts remained after the imperial troops withdrew. A further obstacle to conversion were the Alemanni, the pagan Germanic tribe that crossed the Rhine and settled in the eastern part of the country. Initially fiercely opposed to Christianity, they destroyed whatever churches and monasteries they found.

The first wave of Alemanni crossed the Rhine and settled in Alsace and on the Swiss plateau in 406, after eleven battles with the Romans. We have little documentation as theirs was an oral tradition centered on heroic tales. Initially independent, the Alemanni later sought protection from the Franks and became a part of the Ostrogoth kingdom. The Ostrogoths in turn were conquered by the Christian Franks, who thus also came to govern the Alemanni, although at first, they apparently did not missionize them.

The conversion of the Alemanni was accomplished peacefully and over a long period – not as might be expected, by the bishops (who tended to be responsible for large territories with scattered parishes), but rather through the influence of local monasteries and the lords of large villas, who provided churches and priests for the families who worked their lands. In both the east and west of Switzerland, the pilgrimage places of saints and martyrs played a large role as centers of veneration, healing, and worship.

Switzerland's Missionary Saints

RTE: Can you tell us now about the area's missionary saints?

PDA. MARGARET: Major saints who contributed to the conversion of eastern Switzerland include the Irish saints Columbanus, Gall, and Fridolin[5], as well as the native Swiss saints Otmar and Lucius.

Although St. Columbanus only stayed about two years before moving on to Italy, he made a lasting impression and was remembered for centuries. According to his *Life*, he once came upon some men solemnly gathered in the woods with a keg of beer, a fire, and a kettle. Discovering that they were about

5 Some now believe that St. Fridolin may have come from Gaul instead of Ireland.

Opposite: St. Gall and the bear, St. Gallen, Switzerland.

to make a beer sacrifice to Wotan, he "upset the vessel with such violence that the hoops burst asunder and all the contents were spilt. Overawed by the kindling eye and the majestic presence of the Abbot, the idolaters dispersed without daring to utter a word of protest..."[6] Another version says "with his breath he caused a keg of beer being offered to Wodan to explode and expel the devils in it. He taught them about Christ and many were baptized."[7]

St. Gall, a disciple of St. Columbanus, lived as a hermit in the woods with his disciples, but influenced the entire area south of Lake Constance by his holy life, his ability to preach in the Alemannian language, and through miracles which continued after his repose. A century later, St. Otmar, known for his humility, poverty, and service to lepers, turned the ruins of St. Gall's hermitage into a monastery, and many local men became monks there. The 6th-7th -century monk St. Fridolin lived on an island in the Rhine, where he established monasteries for men and women, and also converted the Alemanni who surrounded him. St. Lucius, probably from east-central Switzerland, proclaimed the faith in the region of Chur.[8]

Another influence in eastern Switzerland were Alemanni who had at first lived in closer proximity to Christian Franks to the west. After their own conversion, some of these anonymous missionaries brought the Christian faith to their eastern brothers, although the process of conversion continued until the early tenth century.

There were many other early saints, such as Sigisbert, Ursanus, Imier, Meinrad and Beatus, who we will describe later.

The Role of Early Monasteries: Fifth-Seventh Centuries

RTE: What can you tell us about the monasteries?

PDA. MARGARET: Monasteries were important in the Christianization of Switzerland, first in the west in the fifth century and later in the east. While early Christian influences were mostly from Roman Italy, in the fifth and sixth centuries, monks and hermits also began coming from Gaul. There,

6 *Life and Writings of St. Columbanus*, p. 187.

7"Die Alemannen und das Christentum." http://www.archaeologie-online.de/magazin/thema/die-alamannen/die-alamannen-und-das-christentum/seite-1/. 1/16/2001.

8 Later legends developed concerning St. Lucius, one of which says he came from Britain.

Opposite: Church of the early medieval Monastery of Romainmotier.

eastern desert monasticism had been absorbed and was then directed back over the Jura mountains to Switzerland via the monasteries of Lérins and Lyon by saints like St. Martin of Tours and Sts. Romanus and Lupicinus of the Jura Mountains. They also brought writings such as *The Conferences and Institutes* of St. John Cassian and Athanasius' *Life of St. Antony of Egypt.*[9] In 450 the monastery of Romanmotier was founded in the Swiss Jura mountains; then in 515, the St. Maurice foundation began in Valais.

In the first half of the seventh century we see at least two monasteries founded by disciples of the Irish St. Columbanus, who had come from his foundation in Luxeil (Gaul) along with his disciple St. Gall. While Columbanus moved on to Italy, Gall lived as a hermit with a small group of followers near Arbon on Lake Constance, later the site of the famous Monastery of St. Gall. In the eighth century, monasteries were founded in eastern Switzerland which not only brought Christian Latin and Greek culture to the Alemanni, but also introduced new agricultural methods in the increasingly settled mountains and forests. In addition to the Monastery of St. Gallen, these were the foundations of Reichenau, Pfäfers, and Rheinau.

These are highlights of the growth of Christianity until the tenth century. Later developments included the tragic dismantling of traditional Christian practices and pilgrimage sites at the Reformation, yet traces of these first-millennium foundations of the universal Church can still be found in Switzerland. ✣

9 Vischer, Lukas; Schenker, Lukas; & Dellsperger, Rudolf, ed., *Ökumenische Kirchengeschichte der Schweiz*, Paulusverlag, Freiburg, Switzerland, 1998, p. 28.

Opposite: Contemporary view of the Monastery of Romainmotier.

Church of St. Maurice Abbey, Saint-Maurice, Switzerland.

II
MARTYRS OF THE SWISS ALPS

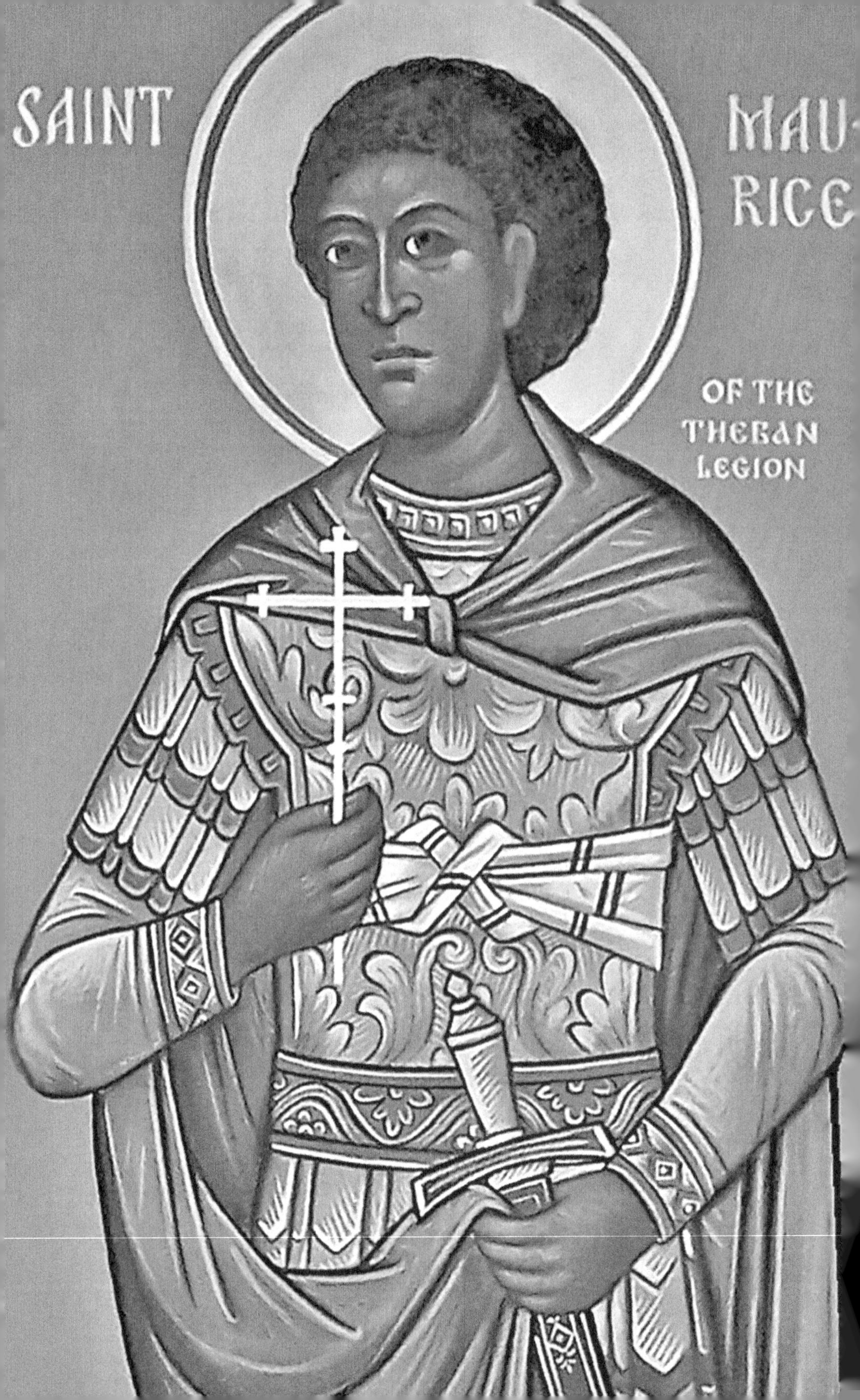
SAINT
MAU-
RICE
OF THE
THEBAN
LEGION

SAINT MAURICE AND THE THEBAN LEGION

By Popadia Margaret Bauman

Saint Maurice and those with him (Sts. Candidus, Exuperius, Felix and Regula, Urs and Victor, and an unknown number of others) were North African legionaries of the Roman army who died for their faith in the mountains of Switzerland. Counted among the great martyrs of the early Church, they are revered by Christians of the Orthodox Church, as well as by Roman Catholics and Copts.

At the time of their martyrdom (around the year 300) people traveled extensively throughout the Roman Empire: merchants brought their wares to far-off regions, and both Roman soldiers and civil servants often served far from their native lands. Thus, for Europeans of the time, the idea of a group of North African martyrs in Switzerland was not as startling as it is to us today.

According to tradition, the Theban Legion was recruited in the Upper Egyptian city of Thebes, about 500 miles south of the Mediterranean, during a period of intermittent persecution of Christians under Roman Emperors Diocletian and Maximian. Blaming those who had abandoned the old Roman gods for the empire's mounting misfortunes, the Romans often punished the refusal to offer sacrifice by execution.

While there are two early accounts of the *passio* or martyrdom of St. Maurice and the Christian members of the Theban Legion, scholars speculate that both originate from an older written or oral tradition. The more detailed account is by St. Eucherius of Lyon, who in the mid-fifth century recorded the events of the martyrdom.

Opposite: St. Maurice, fresco from St. Innocent Orthodox Church, Redford, Michigan.

From Egypt, the Theban Legion was sent to Italy, and then crossed the Alps through today's Great St. Bernard Pass, arriving in southern Switzerland on their way to curb an uprising of Burgundian Vandals who were causing unrest along the Roman frontier. Once through the pass, the legion camped at Agaunum, a Roman post (now the town of Saint-Maurice) along the Rhône River, where they were asked to sacrifice to the Roman gods in preparation for their campaign. Other versions state that they were asked to persecute Christians in Gaul, or that they had already successfully defended the border and were camped in Agaunum for the winter. The traditional story records that Emperor Maximian, encamped nearby, ordered a celebration that included sacrifice to the Roman gods. The legion's Christians refused to sacrifice, and Emperor Maximian ordered that every tenth man be killed. They drew lots and those chosen were decapitated. Their Christian officers, Sts. Maurice, Candidus, and Exuperius, encouraged those who remained to stay strong, but when the emperor found out that they still refused, he repeated the execution of every tenth man. St. Maurice then wrote a letter which appears in Eucherius' account:

> "Emperor, we are your soldiers, but first and foremost we are servants of God. We offer to you our virtue in battle, to Him our innocent life. You pay for our efforts, He granted life to all the world. Even an imperial order does not authorize us to deny our God and Creator, our God who is also your God and Creator, whether you admit it or not. We use our weapons for our compatriots, not against them. We fight on account of our faithfulness to you, but how can we be faithful to you if we fail to offer our faithfulness to God? We first swore allegiance to God, and only afterwards to our general. You could not trust our second oath if we broke the first..."

The incensed emperor then ordered that all remaining Christians in the legion be put to death. Though a small number escaped, the majority were killed, and the martyred legionaries are commemorated by the Church on September 22/October 5.

A full Roman legion contained 6600 men, the number that Eucherius claimed was martyred. However, a portion of a legion was referred to by the

Opposite: Detail of statue of St. Maurice, ca. 1250, Cathedral of St. Maurice and St. Catherine, Magdeburg, Germany.

same name, and there are indications that parts of the larger legion were stationed throughout Italy, in Switzerland, and in Germany. Thus, another source relates that 520 soldiers were martyred in Agaunum/Saint-Maurice. Archeologists have only found six graves. In such early Latin texts, a line over a number multiplied it by a thousand, and it is thought that perhaps an accidental misreading of six became six thousand.

The martyrdom was not the end of the story. Local Christians knew where the martyrs were buried, and came to the place to pray secretly during persecution and publicly once the Edict of Toleration was implemented by Galerius in 311. Sometime after the edict was ratified by St. Constantine the Great and his co-ruler Licinius in 313, hermits moved into the area, which was already regarded as a holy site with, perhaps, a small church built there.

In the fourth century, Bishop Theodore of Octodurus uncovered the relics of the martyrs and moved them about a mile from the martyrdom to a site under a cliff where he built a church and baptistery in what is now the town of Saint-Maurice. This was a period in which the Christian West was greatly influenced by the fathers of the Egyptian desert, and the site Bishop Theodore chose recalled their isolation. In 515, the Burgundian King Sigismund founded a monastery in Agaunum/Saint-Maurice and enlarged the church. Historians believe that there was probably a monastic brotherhood there already, or at least local hermits who formed a community, and the first prayers and services glorifying the martyrs were probably written around this time. Early pilgrims to the grave of St. Maurice included Abbot Romanus of the Jura Fathers, St. Martin of Tours, and St. Athanasius of Egypt.

After the traditional account of the martyrdoms was recorded in the *Passio*, the relics became a major pilgrimage destination. Many were converted, healed of illness, or freed of demonic possession by praying at the graves, and liturgical hymns for the martyrs spread to churches throughout the region, contributing to the conversion of the local population to Christianity.

Eventually, the veneration of St. Maurice and the Theban Legion spread from the place of their martyrdom to Gaul, especially Burgundy, and then throughout Switzerland and Germany, and finally to Italy, where St. Ambrose of Milan promoted the veneration of other Theban Legionaries martyred in Italy. Churches and monasteries in other towns and regions soon enshrined portions of the relics, dedicating new temples and monastic sites to the martyrs.

Opposite: Mosaic altarpiece: Martyrdom of St. Maurice, St. Maurice Abbey.

In the ninth century, Charlemagne drew attention to St. Maurice by describing him as "the ideal knight," and relics of St. Maurice and his martyred soldiers were transferred to Magdeburg (eastern Germany) in 961. Within a few years, the Holy Roman Empire took him as patron of both empire and army. Until the mid-13th century St. Maurice was portrayed as a Caucasian soldier in Roman army dress. The first statue portraying him with African features was carved in the 13th century, and now stands in the Cathedral of St. Katherine and St. Maurice in Magdeburg, Germany. Around the same time, at least two other saints were portrayed as black: St. Gregory the Moor in Cologne, and one of the three kings or magi, whose relics are also ascribed to Cologne.

A Contemporary Pilgrimage to Saint-Maurice

The town of Agaunum (Saint-Maurice), which grew up around the monastery, is small and quite out of the way, though accessible by trains and good roads. Located in the French-speaking part of Switzerland, I was blessed to visit the site with my French-speaking cousin and her husband. Having driven through breathtaking Swiss scenery that included foothills of the Alps and the shore of Lake Geneva, we were welcomed into town by a rainbow overhead, and from our second-story balcony that evening we could see the Church of St. Maurice as a dark bulk rising out of the mist.

The monastery has been in existence from the fourth or fifth century, and the monks still pray the traditional *Laus Perennis*, around-the-clock psalter readings. The monks and clergy minister to people of the area and have a large parochial school for Catholic youth.

Tours of the monastery church and its treasures are available (although a tour in another language than French should be arranged in advance). We arrived for our tour just as an unannounced busload of French schoolchildren pulled up. Our monk-guide dealt with their presence by whisking us off to the treasury room, which opens like a large bank vault, where he locked us in while he spoke with the school children. Here, glass-fronted cabinets contain centuries-old gifts given to the church in honor of the Theban Martyrs, including a reliquary with small fragments from Christ's crown of thorns donated by Charlemagne. On a large central table are three reliquary caskets that are carried in procession on their feastday, containing relics of St. Maurice and his companions.

When the schoolchildren departed, we received our promised tour. The doors of the church have modern relief-work depicting the martyrdom of the Theban Legion, alongside more recent figures such as WWII German resistance workers, Martin Luther King, Jr., Mahatma Gandhi, and the Russian New Martyrs.

Inside the church are stunning modern stained-glass windows that tell the story of the Theban Legion, beginning with their departure from Thebes and ending with the reliquary procession held every year on the martyrs' feast. In front of the sanctuary is a large, magnificent mosaic of St. Maurice, portraying his martyrdom and reception into heaven. (Photo of mosaic, pg. 28.)

Finally, the monk opened up the gift shop, where we found booklets in English and German, and it was only when I read them later that I learned that about a mile outside of town is a small chapel where tradition says the martyrdom took place. A fresco of the martyrdom adorns the chapel walls, and a huge flat stone suspended by ironwork is believed to be the one on which they were executed. Those seeking a blessing or healing may walk or sit under it. The second floor of the chapel once contained living quarters for custodian-hermits, and in earlier centuries there were rooms off the chapel where pilgrims seeking healing could stay during their visit.

The veneration of St. Maurice and the Theban Legion is growing in the United States. On my return, I gave a slide show of my pilgrimage to St. Maurice at the annual Ancient Christianity and African-American Conference, attended mostly by Orthodox Christians who seek racial reconciliation and heavenly intercessors to guide them; a number of people were already familiar with him. (See www.mosestheblack.org). Also, several icons of St. Maurice have recently been painted in the United States and Canada, including the one shown here from St. Innocent of Irkutsk Church in Detroit, Michigan. (Photo of St. Maurice icon, pg. 24.)

In his *Vita Patrum*, St. Gregory of Tours says, "The purpose of the lives of the saints is not to give abstract knowledge but... to edify spiritually and to inspire to imitation." The saints of the Theban Legion continue to fulfill this role by inspiring new peoples of many lands and showing all of us an example of ultimate Christian witness. ✠

SANKT
THEODUL

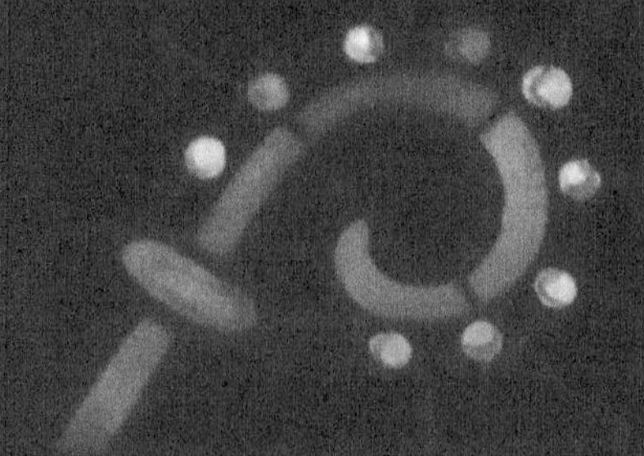
SANKT
MORITZ

THE SWISS LEGACY OF THE THEBAN MARTYRS

by Cornelia Delkeskamp-Hayes

Agaunum and the Theban Legion

On a lovely drive south along Lake Geneva, we find ourselves between the Dents du Midi and the Bernese Alps with their snow-clad summits. The road itself follows the Rhône River, which, confusingly at this point, flows north for a cool bath in Lake Geneva, then arcs around south towards the Mediterranean.

Agaunum (Saint-Maurice) is situated in the Valais Canton, between Geneva and the Simplon Pass into Italy, where we arrive at the Abbey of St. Maurice, tucked at the bottom of a high cliff. The little town consists of a built-over stream (with a highway roaring along in the background) and one lively street whose little restaurants are populated by local families. The La Dent du Midi Hotel in the center offers a quiet lunch on its shady terrace.

The church is not terribly old: after a rockfall destroyed an earlier Baroque church, the present building was erected on a north-south axis. We'd booked a tour of the monastery church, but our guide, lacking knowledge about the saints and sympathy for Christianity in general, reels off unedifying years and meters. Next time we will insist on a tour by the abbot (available on advance booking, probably in French).

The famous baptistery from the fourth or fifth century is so small that full immersion must have been impossible even at that early date, and I wonder if they had already settled for sprinkling. While looking over the church I fail to spot the chapel dedicated to St. Sebastian, where a shrine on a Baroque altar contains relics of the Theban martyrs.

Opposite: St. Theodul elevating Theban relics, Saint-Maurice.

The excavations of the early church erected over a pagan temple to a nymph are closed, nor can the catacombs be visited, although from a high grid floor, we can look down onto 44 graves, accompanied by the sound of 6000 liters of water per minute rushing by underneath. When the train tunnel was built through the mountain, a Roman water pipe was cut, and this is a problem for the abbey's treasure room which now suffers from humidity.

In the Church Treasury

The Abbey of St. Maurice contains Switzerland's most precious collection of church treasure, along with a reliquary shrine for St. Mauritius and busts of Sts. Candidus and Victor. The nice watchwoman alerts me to the martyrs' relic chapel which is hardly noticeable to the casual visitor who focuses on the glittering exhibition. This, finally, is where pilgrims can hold their own services, a quiet place I hadn't found in the busy church. For a short time, I have that special place to myself.

Unfortunately, we miss the lovely St. Sigismund Chapel and his reliquary right next door. This king of Burgundy had converted from the Arian heresy in 500, with all of his people following suit, and he seems to have rebuilt the monastery here as a penance for having killed his first-born son at the instigation of a second wife. He himself and three later sons were eventually drowned by a Frankish Arian king in Orleans, and the monks of St. Maurice enshrined their relics three years later, venerating them as missionaries and martyrs.

From Agaunum we had planned to visit the Theban Legion's place of martyrdom at nearby Vérolliez with its very early chapels, but spectators of the *Tour de France* bicycle race had taken hold of the street in that direction, so we escape onto the highway. Way up on the mountain above the Abbey of St. Maurice, we can see the ruins of a hermitage that was inhabited by Saint Amatus of Grenoble, who became a monk here in 581, and later the bishop of Sitten.

Opposite: St. Maurice Church tower.

Andermatt and Zürich: Sts. Felix, Regula, and Exuperantius

We spend the night in Andermatt in a room right under the roof, very close to the church tower which, unlike the western cantons, keeps up its centuries-old service of marking time every quarter hour. I feel like I am back in my childhood village, where such bells used to keep me awake. The 12th-century church of St. Columbanus is closed for restoration, although relics of the Zürich patron saints, Felix and Regula, and possibly their servant Exuperantius, were moved here to Andermatt to protect them from the ravages of the Reformation. The relics are kept in the sacristy.

A decade ago, Margaret Bauman wrote about her pilgrimage to Zürich to venerate Felix and Regula:

> According to an eighth-century source, Felix and Regula were siblings, and members of the Theban Legion under St. Maurice stationed in Agaunum. When the legion was to be executed in 286, they fled, reaching Zürich before they were caught, tried and executed. After being beheaded, they miraculously got to their feet, picked up their own heads, and praying, walked forty paces uphill before laying down to die. They were buried where they lay, on the hilltop which would become the site of the 12th century *Grossmünster* (Great Minster), built over a Roman burial ground.
>
> Here I was especially shocked at the ravages of the Reformation. I learned that the Reformer Zwingli had gotten rid of the chalices, monstrances, and statues; thrown out the relics of the saints; painted over all of the beautiful frescoes; and torn down the altar tables in this and six other churches to build himself a pulpit from which to preach! The Swiss are now conscious of their losses, at least in the realm of art history, and are trying to uncover the frescoes in the churches and display the remaining church objects in museums.
>
> In 1950 a Catholic church was founded in Zürich in the names of the martyrs, and relics were brought to it from the small town of Ander-

Opposite: Andermatt Church of Sts. Peter and Paul.

matt. These relics had been rescued at the time of Zwingli, when the relics of Zürich's saints were thrown together into a "bone house" (ossuary). However, those of Felix and Regula, the city's patrons, were taken for safekeeping to Andermatt by a local man who was in Zürich at the time.

Another event which brought recognition to the patron saints of Zürich took place in 2004, when all of the Orthodox jurisdictions in town, including four Chalcedonian (Russian, Serbian, Greek, and Romanian) as well as five Oriental Orthodox churches, held a joint vespers service at the Grossmünster on the eve of the feast of Sts. Felix and Regula, and then presented the church with an icon which had been painted of the saints. This icon now hangs in the stairwell leading down to the former burial chapel of the martyrs.

In Solothurn: Sts. Ursus and Victor

In Solothurn, the Aare River is easy to ford, and a late Celtic bridge marks an early settlement. Around 20 AD, a small Roman village was built here that expanded to both sides of the river and, by the mid-third century, had grown into a large settlement with fortifications to withstand the onslaught of migrating Germanic tribes.

Along with sixty-six other Christian soldiers, Sts. Ursus (Urs) and Victor escaped the massacre of St. Maurice and his troops in Agaunum (present-day St. Maurice), but were finally captured and killed in Solothurn in 303. When the Roman governor Hirtacus gave them the choice of sacrificing to the Roman gods or suffering death, they remained steadfast and were sentenced to be burnt on a great bonfire. However, a huge downpour of rain put out the fire. Hirtacus therefore ordered the soldiers to be decapitated on a flat stone placed on the Aare bridge; the bodies were thrown into the river. Their relics washed ashore, where they were secretly recovered and buried at night by local Christians.

The old town of Solothurn is one big pedestrian zone. Only hotel guests with luggage are allowed to drive their cars over the historic cobblestones, so we bump past the Cathedral of St. Urs (also dedicated to Sts. Victor and Ver-

Opposite: Icon of Sts. Urs and Victor. Solothurn Cathedral.

IC XC
S·VIC
TOR·

ena), asking our way to the charming little *Hotel Zum Wirthen*. Here, tourists and townspeople enjoy their evening drink on the sidewalk, and watch with interest our attempts to consolidate suitcases, notebooks, camera, picnic utensils, and laptop into inconspicuous-looking bundles. Our room faces the town's 15th-century clock tower, erected by the canton in order to silence competing church bells ringing out denominationally diverse hours of prayer – a solution that has become the rule in Switzerland. My foreboding is confirmed by another sleepless night: official times are proclaimed without mercy. Twenty-four times a day Solothurnians are treated to a droning secular *memento mori*, as knight, king, and a figure of death make their circling appearance. This 12th-century tower is the oldest edifice in the city, with the astronomical clockwork added three centuries later.

Solothurn's Cathedral of St. Ursus

Early next morning, I am eager to get into St. Ursus. Mighty steps lead up to the open portal and the huge space inside is filled with white stucco. I try to imagine the original Romanesque columned basilica, erected over an earlier memorial building for the saint. Here, a monastic settlement is said to have soon developed. That Ursus and Victor played an important role was first noted in 445 by Eucherius, bishop of Lyon, and author of the first account of the Theban Legion's sufferings. After 600 however, the original monastic cells were abandoned and both memory and veneration of the saints lapsed. Only in 740 did St. Werthrada (Berta), the mother of Charlemagne, revive the place by founding her own monastic dependency. The settlement soon grew into a village for fisherfolk, boatmen, and their families.

The present Baroque-Classicist design is from the 18th century when the complex was rebuilt. A dramatic Baroque Gloriole with a cross in a wreath of clouds dominates a glass sarcophagus with the bones of those who are identified today with the Theban Martyrs. I try to concentrate on the saints, doing my morning prayers in front of two beautifully painted icons.

Saint Peter's Church

The veneration of St. Victor, on the other hand, began at the place of his own *memoria*, situated under another church, a little below the cathedral and

Opposite: Cathedral of St. Ursus. Solothurn, Switzerland.

closer to the river. Today it is called St. Peter's Church. Access is possible (and for me alone) by leaving my passport with the Tourist Office as security for a key.[1] The church lies almost hidden, surrounded by houses for canons and curates of later times.

The present church seems to have been founded in the 10th century by another Berta, the queen and widow of Rudolph II of Burgandy, who was believed to have donated relics of St. Urs. In 1473, foundation work uncovered skeletons of many faithful who had been buried near the saints, and these were boldly identified as relics belonging to other Theban martyrs. (Therefore, relics in Solothurn after that date should be scrutinized with care.) In 1474, a year after this multiplication of Thebans, the original relics of both St. Urs and Victor are said to have been translated to the newly rebuilt Cathedral of St. Ursus. However, the inhabitants of Solothurn seem not to have been aware of that translation, for forty years later when they reworked the cathedral altar and found a sarcophagus with two skeletons, they were quite surprised. One had a silver nameplate designating him as St. Urs, and the other was assumed to be St. Victor.[2] Additionally, a 1973 renovation of St. Peter's high altar has revealed sealed pewter boxes containing relics. Today their relics are said to be located on the back of the altar in a sealed compartment. It is a lovely feeling to have the holy place all to myself, with plenty of time to look around and pray.

Surprisingly, the two saints remained entirely untouched during the Reformation, and once the counter-Reformation was securely established, Christians began distributing relics again. After the secularization following the French Revolution, the bishopric of Basel was reestablished and the bishop's seat moved to Solothurn. Only at that point was the church of St. Urs elevated to the rank of a cathedral. Although the history of veneration here is confusing, surely some of the relics of Urs and his companions are located in the cathedral treasury's reliquary busts that are placed on the altar on high feast days.

1 The policy of handing out keys has now been discontinued. Today one needs to contact the local church authorities in advance to visit St. Peter's.

2 According to one account, the 6th-century Burgundian Princess Sedeleuba translated the relics of St. Victor to a church in Geneva dedicated to him. No traces of the church remain today, however, and with the second skeleton in Solothurn now accepted as that of St. Victor, it seems clear that the relics transferred to Geneva had not been his after all.

Opposite: Image of St. Victor dressed as a medieval Swiss knight.

SCA
VERENA

Saint Verena Gorge

In the afternoon, we drive north toward the foothills, following signs to the *Verenaschlucht* (St. Verena Gorge). A stream glitters through the canyon, skipping over huge stones abutted by towering cliffs. Wooden bridges and shrines with crosses carved into the rock line the route, often with burning candles. There are few visitors in the evening and thankfully, the tourist restaurant next to the hermitage is closed.

Here, outside of Solothurn, St. Verena, an Egyptian woman associated with the Theban Legion, had her hermitage – a two-story cave where she prayed, missionized and healed. The 12th-century St. Martin's chapel was erected in front of the cave, and is open until early afternoon. On the other side of the little stream, built in the opening of a large cave, is a later Gothic style church dedicated to St. Verena. During St. Martin's opening hours, one can look through a small, iron-gridded window into the St. Verena's columned narthex, where a small bust of the saint may contain a relic. To view it we would have had to contact the Solothurn city chancellor before our visit. The "supervisor-hermit" in his small house next to the holy places is not authorized to open the chapel; rather, he is there to preserve the silence of the place. Until the 18th century a monk held this office, and when monks became scarce, laypeople took their place. It was such a beloved position that contests were held to decide who would qualify as successor. After the Reformation, interest in pilgrimage ran dry until the 19th century when visitors increased with the Romantic rediscovery of nature.

Life of St. Verena

Saint Verena is thought to have been a relative of the officer Mauritius (now Saint-Maurice), who served in the Theban Legion. His companion Victor was her fiancé, and to be near him she followed the legion to Milan. When the legionaries marched north over the Alps, Verena stayed in Milan, caring for imprisoned Christians and burying them after their martyrdoms. Hearing about the decapitation of Mauritius and his soldiers in Agaunum (now Saint-Maurice), she traveled there to bury them as well, and afterward continued to Solothurn where her fiancé also met his end.

Opposite: St. Verena icon in Solothurn Cathedral.

Alone and friendless, she found another Christian who had managed to escape from the legion. They moved into the two-story hermitage which can still be seen today. Verena also was befriended by an old Christian woman who sold the girl's handwork so that she could live. Blessed with a gift of healing, Verena was soon recognized as a saint by the neighborhood's pagan Alemanni,[3] and many were converted. Other young women joined her, forming a community. Eventually, the pagan governor imprisoned Verena, until a high fever laid him low. Remembering her reputation as a healer, he had the young woman brought from prison, and when healed he granted her freedom, but exiled her from the region.

Today, Solothurn is the most beautiful Baroque city of Switzerland, a legacy from the 16th-18th centuries when French emissaries to the Swiss Confederation resided here. The stores are exquisite and even late at night we find charmingly quiet squares with open outdoor cafes and sparkling fountains.

Bad Zurzach and St. Verena

The sun still burns down on us as we arrive in tiny Bad Zurzach on the Rhine River, whose famous St. Verena Minster can be mistaken for a stately village church. An impressive information center and museum depict life in an early Roman camp, medieval castle architecture, fairs, the first trains, and streets connecting Bad Zurzach with the world at large.

Bad Zurzach was first called Tenedo, conveniently situated on the Rhine and at the crossroads leading to Avenches, Augst, Zürich, Schleifheim on the Danube, and into Alsace. Here the Romans established a small military camp in 10 BC and later built a new *castellum*, a small Roman fort or tower where Christians are believed to have settled from the second century on. It was only after Stilicho led his Roman army over the Alps around 400 that the camp became a sizable civil settlement, its fortifications serving as the town's walls. In a corner of the walls was an early Christian church dedicated to the Mother of God with a baptistery and a house for the priest.

This, then, is the place where St. Verena ended her days. Living first in Solothurn, and then as a hermit on an island in the Rhine (now the small village of Koblenz),[4] she finally moved to Zurzach, where the priest willingly took her on as his housekeeper.

3 *The Life of St. Verena* errs here – the Alemanni came to the region later; the people in her time were probably Celts.

4 Not the large city of Koblenz at the confluence of the Moselle and the Rhine.

Opposite: St. Verena Minster and Crypt Tower, Bad Zurzach.

Every day Verena, carrying a jug and a comb, would walk from the town to a settlement of lepers and outcasts, to care for the sick and poor. The priest's envious servants rightfully accused the saint of serving the poor with the priest's own wine and bread, but when stopped and questioned, the household wine in her jug had changed to water.

Another miracle concerned the priest's ring. Not wishing to wear precious jewelry during Lent, he gave the ring to Verena for safekeeping. To discredit the saint, another servant stole the ring and threw it into the Rhine. In desperation, Verena begged God's help, and shortly after, a fisherman came to the rectory to present a large, newly-caught fish. When it was cut apart, the ring was found. Later Verena lived as a recluse in her own room until her repose.

A fifth-century church was erected over Verena's grave outside the fortress in a Roman burial ground, and today this grave is in the center of bustling Zurzach. The church was enlarged over time, her grave eventually covered by a remarkable choir tower. On the altar stand two Coptic icons, sent in 2007 from Port Said, depicting Sts. Mauritius and Verena.

Saint Verena's first *vita* was composed in 890 by Abbot Hatto of Reichenau, probably for the edification of the pious empress St. Richardis. An embellished life from the tenth century describes more miracles, one of them turning on a shepherd who found a little stone jug with healing powers in the ruins of the old church in the *castellum*. A chapel dedicated to Verena and Mauritius was erected inside the ruins before 1000, and it can still be seen.

From the tenth century onward, Zurzach became a prominent place of pilgrimage, and St. Verena is still one of the most venerated saints of Switzerland.

I wanted to visit the crypt with its arm relic of St. Verena, usually accessible from the outside of the minster. I also wanted my faithful driver-husband to experience that holy place, offering a little prayer to St. Verena. Although it was only 5:00 pm, long before the official closing time, the door was securely locked. As I searched for help, my husband came searching for me, and I spotted him beckoning from the back of the minster. There he stood, having opened the door without difficulty. Of course, he was convinced that I pulled or pushed where I should have pushed or pulled, but he was wrong. The door was locked, but this is how Michael found himself coming along – even if merely worried that his wife, unable to enter an open door, might not be able to get out by herself.

Opposite: Scene of St. Verena's charity. Bad Zurzach.

Now we are ready for a coffee. I'm aware that the lovely landscaping surrounding the information center with its delicious cakes was created at the cost of history, when the monastery's farm houses and medieval trade buildings were pulled down to further Zurzach's ambitions as a spa. The community must have thought that five churches were enough in the way of ancient architecture, and that visitors would favor flowers.

I realize that I have forgotten to take photos and return for a moment, this time without my husband. It is incredible, but the door is locked again. I go back to the church where one can peer into the crypt, but not well enough for a picture. In the meantime, Michael comes after me, and when I again complain about the locked crypt he doesn't believe a word. As we round the corner, there is the door wide open! He lingers to watch while I take my pictures and silently thank the saint for hearing my prayers.

Vevey: Bishop Amvrosii and a Conversation About the Theban Legion

Margaret Bauman had asked if I might interview Bishop Amvrosii Cantacuzène, who was quite knowledgeable about the Swiss saints and had composed a service in their honor. Bishop Agapit of the Russian Church Abroad in Germany consented to call the retired hierarch on my behalf, and later reported that although the bishop still serves his church in Vevey, he is old and very ill. "Still," he continued, "it would benefit you greatly to try to talk with him."

I called, uncomfortable with my rusty French and imagining a weak invalid at the other end of the line. But instead, we had an exhilarating exchange, the bishop's voice much younger and livelier than I had expected. He emphasized that he was not strong enough for visitors, yet seemed eager to continue our conversation, and in the end set a time for a meeting.

On the appointed day, Vladika Amvrosii welcomed me warmly. As we became acquainted he spoke about growing up as an Orthodox Christian in Vevey. Though of Russian descent, his parents were also born in Switzerland, so he feels quite at home here. He alternates Russian and French services weekly, and about sixty percent of his Russian choir consists of converts for whom Russian is a foreign language.

Opposite: Statue of St. Verena, Bad Zurzach.

He also tells me about the service he has composed to the Swiss saints, and his plans to insert the biblical and patristic proof texts before publishing it. Here is the troparion, translated from German:

> As lovely fruit of your saving seed, O Lord,
> Helvetia offers you the multitude of her saints,
> who have grown forth from her soil.
> May You guard your church in our lands in deep peace
> through their prayers and the power of Thy cross,
> O gracious All-Merciful One!

I tell Vladika of our visit to St. Ursanne and Saint-Imier in the Jura mountains, of the palpable presence of St. Urs, and his continuing veneration in St. Ursanne, but also of the disappointing neglect of the architectural and spiritual heritage of St. Imier's founder. The bishop fills in details about St. Imier, and how the many relics he brought back from Jerusalem had made his hermitage so attractive to pilgrims: "At first, people came to venerate the relics, then they stayed to talk to the saint, but in the end, they came for his pastoral care."

Vladika does not have much patience for the doubts which have been raised in recent years about the existence and martyrdom of the Theban Legion in Augunum/Saint-Maurice. First, he argues that in times of underdeveloped literacy one can trust oral tradition. Second, he agrees with historians that no Theban legion had been levied from Egypt and transported over the Alps before the recounted martyrdoms in Augunum. In fact, the 10th and 11th Legions were stationed in Milan for quite some time, and only later sent north to settle the Danube border. Moreover, the bishop explains their martyrdom at a time when general persecution was no longer in force by an unfortunate accident: When Emperor Maximian passed through the area, he decided to visit the troops and reward their successful defense of the border with an official celebration. It was this celebration which included the usual pagan ritual sacrifices, and thus exposed the Christian soldiers when they refused to participate.

The bishop's third argument is particularly important. Vladika believes that the Egyptian origin of the martyrs is established by the witness of Saint Athanasius of Alexandria, who is said to have made a detour on one of his journeys to Gaul to venerate the relics of his compatriots. The journeys in question must have occurred between 342 and 345, and I can only hope that someone more knowledgeable than myself will at some point work through the bishop's papers and find his sources.

At any rate, these findings caused Vladika to place St. Athanasius at the side of Saint Irenaeus of Lyon (along with the Apostle Barnabas who is believed to have gone to Milan, Vladika's own namesake, St. Ambrose) an icon he asked to be painted of the saints of Switzerland. Although they did not all live here, each of these saints had a significant role in the Christianization of Switzerland.

A newer version of the icon includes Saint John Maximovitch of Shanghai and San Francisco, who was Vladika Ambrosii's predecessor on the episcopal throne in Geneva. Saint John celebrated in Vevey, and Bishop Amvrosii is convinced that he still takes care of the Swiss Orthodox Church today. (Saint John's icon in the church contains a small relic.) He then goes on to tell me about a 12th-century church in Zillis (Graubünden) that features 153 Swiss saints frescoed on the ceiling.

Our exchange touches on the subject of ecumenism, which the bishop regards with a reserve based in history: Beginning with Charles Martel, the Carolingians had sent missionaries to Saxony, who prayed the Filioque addition to the Nicean Creed. Vladika fully sympathized with my own initial difficulties in regard to St. Boniface. In spite of the saint's enormous achievements for the Christian mission in Germany, he focused on streamlining all Christian practices to those endorsed by Rome, in particular enforcing the principle of a celibate clergy. In the end, Bishop Ambrosii followed the guidance of St. John Maximovitch and his recommendation to go ahead and venerate all of the pre-schism saints of Europe.

As I was informed later, the following night saw the completion of Bishop Amvrosii's service on earth. Memory Eternal! May he rest in peace with his beloved saints. ✠

Benedictine Abbey of Einsiedeln.

III
MISSIONARY SAINTS OF SWITZERLAND

LORENZ

IN THE COMPANY OF SWISS SAINTS

by Cornelia Delkeskamp-Hayes

Sion (Sitten): Sts. Amatus, Theodul, and Altheus

We depart from Agaunum/Saint-Maurice onto the highway that leads to Sitten, now called Sion. On the mountain above the abbey, we can see the ruins of a hermitage once inhabited by St. Amatus of Grenoble, who became a monk here in 581, and later the bishop of Sitten. He also founded his own double monastery in Remiremont, with nuns on a Vosges mountaintop and monks in the valley below.

With the Rhône River and Bernese Alps to the left and the Wallis Alps on the right, we reach Sitten with its two, steep fortress-bedecked hills framing the old city. One of the oldest bishop's seats in Switzerland, the town is surprisingly small, but boasts of lovely historical integrity.

The place had been settled since the Stone Age, and in 580, the bishopric was moved here from Martigny for better protection against barbarian invasions. The relics of the saintly bishop Theodul (also called Theodor or Joder) were also translated. In the eighth or ninth century, an austere church dedicated to him was built over an Arcosol grave (a trough hewn in rock, covered by a vaulted niche), the first resting place of the relics. In 1200, the relics were transferred to the Valeria Basilica on one of the town's hills, but lost during the French occupation of 1789. Veneration of this saint was widespread in the Alpine region, and the Bavarian monastery of Ottobeuren displays a very elaborate reliquary attributed to the saint in its Sts. Alexander and Theodor church. It is a lovely walk in the evening sun up to the Valeria fortress, church, and ruins of the bishop's palace.

In Sitten there is also a cathedral treasury with the relics of St. Altheus, a later abbot of St. Maurice Monastery (786-804) and bishop of Sitten. Perhaps this is the source of the holiness that this place breathes.

Opposite: Remains of Valeria Fortress and Basilica, Sion (Sitten).

Disentis: St. Sigisbert

The name Disentis derives from the Latin *desertina*, a deserted place, and such solitude and mild climate were sought out around 700 by St. Sigisbert, a pupil of St. Columbanus, who dedicated his own church to the Frankish St. Martin of Tours.

Sigisbert found a powerful sponsor in the Disentis' landowner Placidus, who was subsequently murdered by a neighboring ruler named Victor, who saw Placidus' support of a Frankish monastic settlement as a threat to his own position. His hasty deed backfired, however, when St. Sigisbert erected a chapel in Placidus' honor at the place of his death, proclaiming him a martyr. In time, Placidus' relics were transferred to the monastery's second church, dedicated to St. Peter, where Sigismund was also buried. Some years later the relics were moved to the crypt of the larger and newly-built St. Martin's church: the generous stipends that Victor was forced to pay the diocese to atone for the murder had been used to enlarge the very monastery he sought to destroy.

Having adopted the Benedictine Rule, the monks cultivated the ground, offered pastoral support for the surrounding area and established a German-speaking school for the Raetian youth. In this way, they qualified the boys for careers within the Frankish administration, which was reasserting its hold on the area. The monastery's position on an important shortcut to Italy would make it a popular stopping place for later Carolingian and German nobles, as well as a hospice for pilgrims. Sadly, after the Reformation and later French secularization, nothing but "ruins and debt" remained. The monastery stayed open, but could no longer accept novices. Finally, around 1880 the locals changed their minds about the benefits they had reaped from the atheist Enlightenment and supported a revival of monastic life and the monastery school.

Today, the monastery's white elongated buildings decorate the mountainside, and the abbey has returned to an earlier model of using the church nave as one side of the monastic square. The main and side naves of the church are about the same height, giving the interior a hall-like character, marked by wall columns where small chapels offer a bit of privacy. The reduced height of the choir and its columns create an impression of great distance. Later, I learn from the monastery's custodian that there are reliquaries of the arms of Sts. Sigisbert and Placidus behind doors to the right and left of the high altar.

Opposite: Disentis and its hillside abbey dedicated to St. Martin.

Having read about the existence of a crypt, I decide to ask if it is accessible. The custodian asks me to wait, and after some time a monk appears who takes me through the gate, down a long hall, and into the monks' private chapel, where in a glass niche below a modern altar rest two pieces of bone of the saints on a red pillow. The chapel benches face a glass wall, behind which are the exposed ruins of the excavated chapel – a marvelous placement as one feels right in the midst of the early remains. Neither the travel guide for the churches of Graubünden nor the local church booklet mention this.

Cazis: St. Victor of Tomils and Cazis

In Cazis, one of the oldest convents north of the Alps awaits us, built by Bishop Victor II of Chur around 700 as a proprietary monastery for educating young relatives and accommodating older unmarried ones. Already active during Roman times and a noted center of early Christian culture, the monastery was originally dedicated to St. Peter and situated in a field close to the seventh-century parish church of St. Martin. The monastery's rigid dependence on the bishops of Chur would have deprived this place of the rich donations other monasteries received from nobles and rulers traveling south in return for protection and supplies.

After its founding, the nuns lived as enclosed canonesses, without vows and entitled to keep their personal property, until the 12th century, when they adopted the cenobitic Augustinian Rule. The Reformation condemned the monastery to a slow demise by forbidding new novices, but with the Counter-Reformation in 1647, the foundation was renewed by Dominican nuns who founded a successful boarding school that still exists. By 1928, economic survival forced the sisters to abandon monastic seclusion and they took outside jobs in schools, kindergartens, and old peoples' homes. Today, they offer retreats in the guest house, and their own bread and ceramics are for sale.

The turbulent history of the monastery left the nuns with few treasures, but one they protect (and even shroud with silence in the monastery guides) are the relics of St. Victor of Tomils and Cazis. Born in 840 in the village of Tomils northeast of Cazis, the priest was unfortunate enough to possess a family vineyard in a very favorable spot. A local nobleman confiscated the land, and when Victor appealed the theft and censured the nobleman's unchristian lifestyle, the priest's head was promptly struck off. At the hour

Opposite: Dominican Convent, built circa 700 in Cazis.

of his death the priest's sisters, both nuns in Cazis, saw a vision of their brother ascending to heaven on a cloud of light. When they learned the circumstances of his death, they took their knowledge as a sign from God and transferred their brother's relics to Cazis. Many miracles occurred in Tomils and Cazis when local people asked for St. Victor's help, and Tomils built a chapel in his memory.

I had heard that St. Victor's relics are behind the Cazis church's high altar, but not wanting to presume, I find two women piling fresh black earth onto a new grave in the cemetery, and ask if I may walk behind the altar. They cheerfully welcome my appearance and answer: "My, yes, go to the saint and tell him to hurry and come back soon." I find the relics behind the altar, beautifully enshrined on red velvet in a glassed-in niche.

The Monastery Kitchen

The cheerful gravediggers next point me to the convent for more information.[1] From the moment I enter, I sense love in this place and understand the source of the kindness shown by the village women. This is the first time that I have ever stepped into a convent, and I begin to understand why Margaret likes being with nuns so much; it is as though one has entered the sitting room of a very dear friend. The guest-nun is not at home, so Sister Renate calls Sister Bernardina, whose white habit has a blue apron attached with a safety pin. Both rummage through old closets and climb up on chairs to search the top shelves for more booklets, but without success. During the search, we talk about the monastery's situation. There are many sisters, and some of them are revitalizing the now extinct Bludenz Monastery, an act of kindness returned, for in the 17th century it was nuns from Bludenz who resettled Cazis.

They tell me the story of their own sisterhood. In the early 13th century, St. Dominic was charged with setting Rome's assorted convents straight. This involved moving the Benedictines of Trastevere into the Dominican reformed monastery of San Sisto Vecchio. The Benedictine nuns were less than enthused, but finally promised to comply if their icon of the Mother

1 Parking in front of the parish church of Sts. Peter and Paul, you can miss the convent, which is right next door, but easily seen approaching from the south. Close by, abutting an old barn (or its successors), is a 12th-century chapel dedicated to the German Saint Wendelin who is perennially popular for his help against animal diseases.

Opposite: View of Cazis, north of the Alps.

of God, attributed by them to the Apostle Luke, would consent. They would carry her to the new place and if she stayed with them in San Sisto (because, as we all know, icons sometimes wander away), the nuns would accept the reform. That seems to have worked out, and today that same icon is preserved and venerated in Rome's Church of Santa Maria del Rosario on Monte Mario.

Chur: Sts. Asinio, Lucius, and Valentian

Four hours from Cazis is the town of Chur, whose early settlements lay on the southwest side of the Plessur River. In the fourth century, the inhabitants withdrew to the opposite bank for protection from invading Alemanni. Shielded by the walls of a Roman *castell* and fortified mountains, Chur preserved its Christianity and strategic position as the only route into Italy.

The first known bishop here, Saint Asinio (consecrated around 451), as well as succeeding bishops, were subject to the ecclesiastical authority of Milan. This connection was advantageous for the acquisition of relics from Milan, which sanctified the first churches of the city, but this link was cut after Charlemagne's death, when Chur-Raetia was joined to the Frankish imperial church and subjected to Mainz.

At the charming Square of St. Martin, the Gothic church dedicated to St. Martin (successor to a Carolingian structure) has become Reformed Protestant: not even a single cross is on display. We climb the stairs through the tower gate to the Bishop's Court (on the site of the Roman *castellum*), which had a measure of legal immunity that kept the diocese from ruin when the Reformation was adopted "downstairs". Although physically preserved, the Bishop's Court only resumed real life in 1848 when Switzerland's federal constitution allowed Catholics once again to move into Chur, where they used the old cathedral as their parish church.

Inside is an astounding Romanesque basilica with early Gothic transept crossings between the nave and the elevated choir, starkly contrasted by cubes of white marble serving as an altar, ambo, and seats. The crypt houses a much later post-schism saint and there seems to be nothing in this church for us. Yet I feel a deep peace and prayerfulness that roots me to my place until we are motioned out.

Opposite: Church of St. Martin, Chur.

Later I read in the guidebook that under the east end of the nave of the present Cathedral of St. Mary of the Assumption are the remnants of a fifth-century choir, rebuilt in the eighth century. The deacon, whom I ask after mass the next morning, unfortunately knows nothing, while the priest does not seem to care even about Sts. Lucius and Emerita, although both are represented on the carved Gothic altar: he insists that they are both legendary. Even more unfortunately, there is no longer a cathedral museum, and the church's treasures are locked up with other cultural remnants of the canton until a new museum can be built. I wonder if the presence of holiness in this place might be due to relics hidden for centuries under the fifth-century choir.

Church of St. Lucius of Chur

Further up on the mountainside, the Church of St. Lucius seems scaled down to modern slimness. Access is possible via the attached seminary. At the time of our visit, the seminary was enveloped by scaffolding, and unfortunately, the doors to the church were closed without explanation. All we could do was enjoy the lovely view into the Rhine Valley.

The life of St. Lucius has been overgrown by many legends. A descendant from the local tribe of the Pritanni, he must have served as a missionary to the pagan populace during a time when there were already Christians in Raetia. Lucius probably worked around the environs of Chur, especially in the Mars Wood, where an early medieval church still remains. Another saint, Emerita, is usually associated with Lucius as a sister, though historians now assign her to the 10th or 11th century.

Up to the 16th-century Reformation there was also a second church to the north of St. Luzius, dedicated to St. Stephen, the First Martyr. The church's untouched late Roman Christian grave chamber was erected over another grave, possibly that of an early bishop such as Asinios. It is currently inaccessible because of construction work, although the barrel-vaulted chamber is supposed to be the largest and most eminent north of the Alps. In 500, a church was built over the chamber with access from the outside for pilgrims. Relics included bones of St. Stephen, whose remains were discovered in 415 in Jerusalem and distributed throughout the Roman Empire, including Milan by 431. Although early, these relics may indeed have been genuine, particularly in an area with strong ecclesiastical links to Milan.

Opposite: Tower of Cathedral Church of St. Mary of the Assumption, Chur.

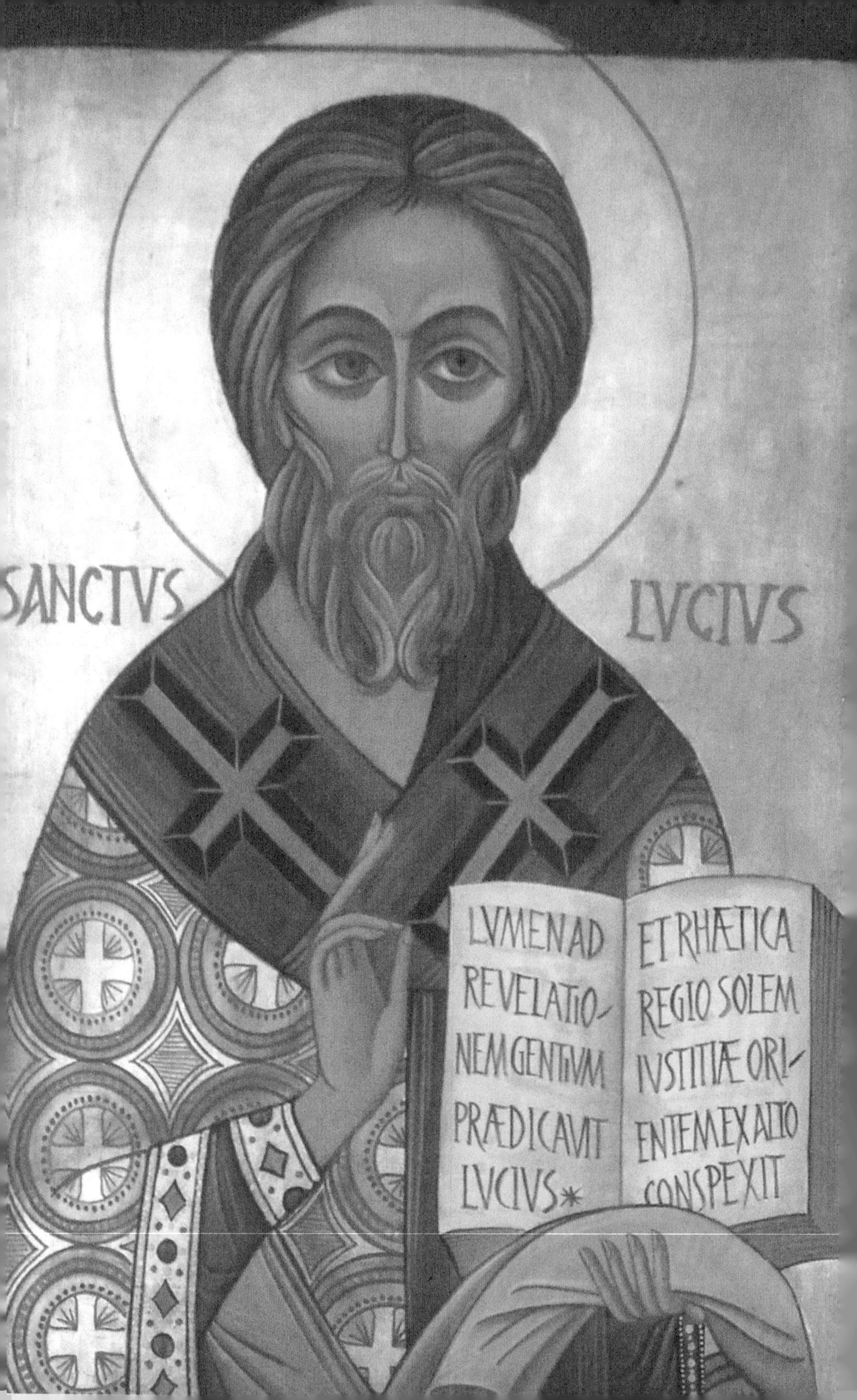

SANCTVS LVCIVS

LVMEN AD
REVELATIO-
NEM GENTIVM
PRÆDICAVIT
LVCIVS *

ET RHÆTICA
REGIO SOLEM
IVSTITIÆ ORI-
ENTEM EX ALTO
CONSPEXIT

The Church of St. Lucius itself was built in 1295, on top of a still older St. Andrew *memoria* built to house relics that had come from Milan prior to 386. When the church was erected, the Apostle Andrew was still the primary patron of the area, long before the veneration of Sts. Lucius and Emerita.

The guide in St. Lucius explains that there was a second burial place under the church for another early bishop, probably a St. Valentian, who had excelled in charity during the barbaric invasions of the sixth century. Later, in the Carolingian period, Victor, the nobleman we mentioned earlier who murdered Placidus of Disentis, used the church as a family burial place. Eager to obtain additional relics, but off-track in his attempt to recover good religious standing, he ordered his disciple, a priest named Otmar, to travel to St. Gallen and to steal St. Gall's relics. However, Otmar's horse (disapproving of the project) threw him off, so that Victor had to settle for the next-best solution of translating the relics of the holy missionary Lucius into this church. Lucius' relics attracted many pilgrims: another case of God's bringing good out of evil!

The church surprises with a simple wooden ceiling. The arrangement is similar to that of the cathedral, but here the view into the vaulted Romanesque crypt is unobstructed, and the visitor feels drawn along the nave and down the central stairs towards the crypt. Underneath the choir, along a small tunnel, is an altar with the reliquary shrine. Sadly, the remarkable bust reliquary of 1252 is part of the church's treasures that need to be locked away, although in the crypt I happily discover an icon of St. Lucius.

Beside the church, in a little house like a porter's lodge, I hope to get change to buy a guidebook. When I ring the bell, a friendly woman appears. As it turns out, she is an Orthodox Christian and the wife of Father Alexandru Dan, the local Romanian priest. He has been here for five years working on a doctoral thesis on the theological differences between the Carolingians and Orthodox (an area of great interest for me), while nurturing his fledgling Romanian parish. His wife already has a doctorate in theology, and as we go on, we discover common friends in Romania. It is suddenly as though I am among dear relatives. Father Alexandru is convinced that the relics of St. Lucius are still under the altar of the cathedral.

Opposite: Icon of St. Lucius from the crypt chapel in Chur.

Saint-Ursanne: St. Ursanus

After Basel, we follow the windings of the Birs River into the Jura Mountains, hidden under heavy grey clouds. Approaching Saint-Ursanne (Ursitz in German) along the Doubs River, we brave a single-lane mountain road with lorry traffic thundering past from the quarry ahead. We enter through St. Peter's gate, which leads right into the central square. Saint-Ursanne is dotted with cafes and ateliers of local artists – jewelry, paintings, and sculptures geared to high-level tourism, but on a weekday, it is peaceful and quiet, even a little sleepy. Brochures are available at a tourist kiosk, and we discover attractive little squares with fountains, rows of trees, and tall painted 16th-century houses.

Life of St. Ursanus

Saint Ursicinus (or Ursanus) lived here as a hermit around 600. According to his *Life* written in the 11th-century, Ursanus was a disciple of St. Columbanus and had followed him from Luxeuil to the land of the Alemanni. Perhaps like St. Columbanus, St. Gall and St. Sigisbert, he was also from Ireland. At first, he preached at Lake Biel, later withdrawing to the obscurity of the Clos du Doubs, with only the ruins of a Roman villa nearby. He practiced his asceticism in a cave in the rock, joined by a bear who became his companion (and possibly a welcome source of winter heat). His holiness and miracles soon drew other monks to him. Saint Ursanus is said to have built the first church in the valley, which was dedicated to St. Peter and served as a parish church until the 19th century, when the building fell to ruin. After the saint's repose, his companion Wandregisel (Wandrille) is thought to have formed a *cella*, a settlement for the brothers, near St. Peter's church. As early as 675, the holy Abbot Germanus of Granfelden also dedicated a church to St. Ursanus next to the bishop's own monastery.

The monastery that developed in Saint-Ursanne adopted the Benedictine Rule, but in the 11th century was transformed into a community of canons. Later, a new abbey church was built next to St. Peter's, which continued to serve the village that surrounded the monastery. Relative peace throughout the 16th century brought economic success, although both town and abbey were devastated a century later in the Thirty Years War. The 18th century

Opposite: View from St. Ursanus cell into the valley.

saw conflicts of power between bishop and canons that prepared the way for clerics' embracing Enlightenment ideals. When these ideals materialized in the French Revolution, the Catholic population sadly did not have much reason to regret the ensuing secularization of the monastery, after which the abbey church served as the village parish and St. Peter's fell to ruin.

The Abbey Church (Collegiale)

I walk the length of the abbey church over a graveled square shadowed by plane trees. One feels it to be a holy place and the 12th-century Gothic structure is highlighted in colors of delicate grey-pink; its Baroque interior has enough space to wander in unobtrusively. The oldest part of the church is the choir with its remarkable *trompe-l'œil* window paintings. Beneath the choir is the beautifully frescoed crypt with Romanesque columns, built as a shrine for the sarcophagus of the saint, which was moved to the high altar and today rests in front of it. There is a small window in the wall of the crypt offering a view of the sarcophagus. The famous gold and silver reliquary-bust seems to be enshrined elsewhere, and can be seen by making arrangements in advance.

Saint Pierre/Saint Peter Church

Next to the lovely late Gothic cloister are the remains of the Church of St. Peter built by St. Ursanus. Excavations below the church have brought to light a group of large stone sarcophagi from the 7th-11th centuries, as many Christians wanted to be buried close to the saint. Today, the church has been restored as a *lapidaire*, a museum for ancient carved stone remnants. The reconstructed cloister is used for art exhibits, underscoring the modern practice of reframing a holy place as a cultural remnant.

The Saint's Hermitage

We hoped to locate the site of the saint's hermitage, and following advice from the tourist kiosk to "go up behind the Collegiale," we find ourselves scrambling through overgrown vineyards. Along the way, we discover many caves with crosses inside – refuges for long-forgotten hermits – but eventu-

Opposite: Abbey church (Collegiale), St. Ursanne.

ally have to admit ourselves lost amidst the brambles. Locals direct us back to St. Paul's gate in the city wall, where a nice Baroque entrance leads up 180 steps past caves and old rebuilt chapels to the hermitage-grotto, decorated with sculptures of the saint and his friendly bear. One can sit there and enjoy St. Ursanus' own view of the silent valley.

Unfortunately, we have no time left to visit the nearby relics of St. Germanus of Granfelden in Delemont (Delsberg), the sacristy that contains his bishop's staff, or the famous monastery of Moutier-Grandval. As we drive away, we enjoy a magnificent view of the town from beyond the river, with a cross rising above the hermitage peak, as if to say that holiness is rooted here.

Saint-Imier: Apostle of the Northern Jura

Saint Imier (or Imerius) was one of the great, even exemplary saints and missionaries of Switzerland although, unfortunately, his relics dwell in a disappointing place. The sixth-century "apostle of the Northern Jura mountains" was from a noble family, and after giving his possessions to the poor, he moved with his servant Albert into the valley which today bears his name. The friends first tilled a small field to support their simple pious lifestyle, and Imier eventually undertook a pilgrimage to the Holy Land, where the patriarch of Jerusalem recognized his gift for languages and kept him on as a secretary. When he returned, Imier continued to live in the place of his earlier labors. Cutting off a branch from a tree and sticking it in the earth, he caused a healing spring to pour forth. Today, the well of that former spring still exists, but lies abandoned, dried out, and forgotten at the side of a busy road.

Soon the saint built a church dedicated to St. Martin of Tours and attracted brothers who formed a monastic community.[2] The present church on the site, still dedicated to St. Martin and built over the grave of St. Imier, was rebuilt three times before 1500, indicating a long-lasting and healthy settlement. In the 16th century, the community was persuaded by the neighboring diocese of Biel to adopt Calvinism. St. Imier's original church, which served the few remaining Catholics, fell apart with time and decreasing attendance, and only the tower remains today. The church nave was turned into a mill by the Protestants, and today serves as a cultural center. A surprisingly pointed modern fresco on the wall of the opposite house shows the saint against

2 See remarks about this early period in Part I, "Over the Alps".

Opposite: Tower of the old St. Imier Church.

VEILLEZ CAR VOVS NE SCAVEZ A QVELLE
HEVRE DOIT VENIR VOSTRE SEIGNEVR

a background of religious ruins, beckoning into a deserted landscape of roughly hewn cubes, with businessmen in suits walking away, supervised by a Santa Claus on TV. The lovely Romanesque abbey church has been exhaustively refashioned according to Reformed principles.

Einsiedeln: St. Meinrad

Einsiedeln, the place of St. Meinrad's labors, was originally covered by dark, pathless woods, which disappeared from view over the years of his sanctifying influence. Today, such rustic landscape can only be summoned by using one's imagination to block out the modern buildings and the many tourists who flock to the city.

Saint Meinrad was born around 800 in the vicinity of Rottenburg to a family of lesser nobility and educated at the famous Benedictine monastery school on the island of Reichenau in Lake Constance. Here his uncle, Erlebald, served as a teacher and later became the monastery abbot. At his uncle's prompting Meinrad was ordained to the priesthood, and in 823 Erlebald advised his nephew to become a Benedictine.

Unlike the other monks who devoted themselves to cultural work in the service of the Carolingian empire (mostly copying and illustrating the famous Reichenau manuscripts), Meinrad preferred a life of asceticism based on St. John Cassian's experience with the desert fathers of Egypt. In spite of this, his uncle sent him to a small metochion situated at Lake Zürich in Babinchova, close to the village of Benken, where he served for some time as principal of the monastery school. In 828, Meinrad finally received permission to live as a solitary on the Etzel pass overlooking the southern shore of the lake, where he built his first hermitage. Today a Baroque chapel marks the place.

Soon his cell became crowded with people seeking the hermit's guidance, and he moved deeper into the woods where, assisted by his monastic brothers and Abbess Heilwiga of Säckingen monastery, he built a chapel, huts for visitors, and his own remote retreat where two ravens kept him company. In 861, after three decades of asceticism, brigands approached his hut, intending to rob him. Meinrad fed them, and understanding their intent, disclosed their plans aloud. Frightened, the brigands murdered the holy man, took his scant belongings, and fled. However, the two ravens followed them, croaking loudly until they reached Zürich, where the criminals were captured and

Opposite: Monastery of St. Meinrad. Einsiedeln, Switzerland.

beheaded. This is why, even now, Einsiedeln has two ravens in its coat of arms. Meinrad's relics were later transferred to the Reichenau monastery.

In spite of the holy man's demise, the monks in the "dark wood" multiplied. In 906, a Strasbourg canon named Benno moved here, and though he was later cruelly blinded by political opponents, he refused the king's offer of an abbey where he could be cared for, moving instead into Meinrad's old hermitage to guide the monks until his repose. As early as 934, Eberhard, a former provost of Strasbourg and a relative of Benno's, transformed the cell into a hermitage, and built a church and monastery with himself as its Benedictine abbot.

In 947, Abbot Eberhard (also venerated as a saint) received relics of Felix and Regula, the patron saints of Zürich, and these are still said to be present in Einsiedeln. There is also speculation that Meinrad's relics were transferred here from the island of Reichenau, and it is suggested that a piece of his skull is enshrined in the back of the altar. There may also be relics here from earlier altars, but it is not clear which saints are enshrined in which altars. There is also a Meinrad altar in the crypt which may contain his relics, but the crypt is inaccessible.

The site of the original monastery chapel survives today in the narthex as a chapel devoted to the Mother of God. Surrounded by pilgrims, the compact black marble structure with its brocaded black Madonna seems to be a place of many miracles. ✣

Opposite: Countryside Chapel of St. Meinrad on the site of his early hermitage near Bollingen, Switzerland.

MARIASTEIN MONASTERY AND THE BASEL RELICS

By Pda. Margaret Bauman

On my first trip to Europe to investigate the early Church in 2001, I was able to go to Basel, Switzerland, my mother's hometown and a beautiful old city on the Rhine River where France, Germany and Switzerland come together. I had first been introduced to its charms as a twenty-year-old student, when a cousin gave me a walking tour of its interesting old houses, and I spent the night in his parents' home on the Rhine, listening to the foghorns on the barges that floated downriver from Rotterdam.

Now, eight years later, my first stop was at the Münster, the former cathedral next to the Rhine whose colorful roof shows up in most pictures of the city. It was formerly a Catholic church dedicated to the Virgin Mary and St. Pantalus, the first bishop of Basel, but is now a Reformed Church and I found it disappointingly plain. I saw this starkness over and over again in Zürich, Romainmotier, and other places – the Reform movement of the 16th century had stripped the church bare of everything dear to the heart of a traditional Christian. I didn't expect icons, but where were the frescoes? the statues? the relics? Even, who is the patron saint of the church?

An earlier search for holy sites had led me to another church in Basel, this one converted to the Historical Museum on Barfüsser Platz. Here was everything that had once been in the churches, even a number of beautiful reliquaries! Later I learned that at the beginning of the 19th century, all of the relics that had landed in the Basel treasury after the Reformation were taken out of their cases, and the archivist was told to either throw them into

Opposite: The Rhine River with the Basel Cathedral in the background. Basel, Switzerland.

the Rhine River or to burn them! He couldn't bring himself to do either, so he carefully labeled and stored each relic. Later he gave them to a Benedictine monastery outside of town, where they were arranged and decorated by local nuns, and where many of the relics can be seen today. So the museum has the empty cases, and the monastery is honoring the real treasures – the precious bones of the saints!

In 2009, I went to Mariastein, the Benedictine Monastery which had received the Basel relics, with my Swiss cousin and a young friend. We took a streetcar from the Basel train station to the outlying town of Flüh, and just before we got out, had a friendly exchange with a local man on how to find the monastery.

A lovely half-hour hike uphill in the rain led us to the monastery church. On both the north and south altars were displays of many relics, each labeled with the saint's name. Since I couldn't read all of the names from where I was standing, I asked a monk if these were the relics from Basel and if there was a listing of them. Before I knew it, we were speaking with another monk, the monastery historian – the very man we had met in the streetcar and the same monk who had written the article about the relics that had brought me here! He showed us materials from the archives and the beautifully handwritten list of all the Basel relics, signed by the abbot who had received them in 1835. Among them were relics of St. Martin, St. Ursula, St. Pantalus, St. Fridolin, St. Verena, and the Apostle Philip, plus many others (a total of ninety-one relics).

The Mariastein Monastery is the second-most visited pilgrimage site in Switzerland after Einsiedeln, commemorating a miracle that happened in the 14th century when a young boy fell 150 feet off the cliff where the monastery is located onto a flat rock, and was saved in the arms of the Virgin Mary. A pilgrimage chapel was built, and in 1540 a second identical accident happened in which another child was also unharmed. Today you can climb down the fifty-six steps leading to the rock, and view the many ex-votos given in thanksgiving for intercession by the Mother of God. ✣

Opposite: Ursula Shrine with relics of the saints of Basel. Mariastein Monastery, Flüh, Switzerland.

PILGRIMAGE TO THE BEATUS CAVES

by Pda. Margaret Bauman

This morning we set out for the Beatus Caves, the traditional hermitage of St. Beatus who converted the area around Beatenberg in the Interlaken District. The caves lie along the famous Pilgrim's Way to St. James at Compostelo, and I had added them as a highlight of my 2014 trip. Although it is difficult to find the best place to enter the Pilgrim's Way or to determine how steep the ascent actually is, I was prepared to go alone by train and boat and then hike up. Fortunately, my friend Cornelia Delkeskamp-Hayes was able to come as well, and early one morning we arrive at Lake Thun (*Thuner See*) to await the boat.

The foggy morning casts a blue haze that makes almost everything invisible; the only definable objects are bright red geraniums hanging in boxes on the side of the pier. Two startlingly black loons suddenly glide into view, followed by our boat, which seems to appear out of nowhere. We climb up to the open deck to watch the fog nesting in the mountains that ring the lake; a Swiss village hugs the shore below. In awe of our surroundings, we speak softly, and traces of French, German, Swiss-German and Chinese waft over the deck. As the day emerges, we make out more of the lovely scenery until finally we see our destination: a sheer cliff with scattered groupings of pine trees rising out of the fog. Are we to climb that?

We debark at Beatenbucht, preferring the stretch of the Pilgrim's Way that takes ninety minutes to the caves, rather than a longer hike from Interlaken. The first few steps are so steep that I wonder if I can make it. My body slowly adjusts, and suddenly the path merges into a wider road – the steep part is only the cut to reach the actual Pilgrim's Way, and from here it is quite manageable.

Opposite: Cornelia Delkeskamp-Hayes awaiting the boat at Lake Thun.

Along the way, a group of happy twelve-year-old Swiss school children come hiking towards us, and as they pass, greet us in Chinese! Several such groups go by, some speaking to us in their native Swiss-German, and others in languages they are learning. They tell us that they are hiking by themselves to a further village: in Switzerland schoolchildren regularly have "*Wandertage*" (hiking days) with their teachers, and these are experienced enough to hike on their own, their teachers meeting them at the other end.

As we ascend the trail, the scenery is spectacular and sometimes frightening: to our left are woods and cliff, to the right a sheer drop-off to the lake. I find that I cannot look down unless I am on the far side of the path. The little red signs soon change from "*Pilgerweg*" (Pilgrimage Way) to "*Wanderweg*" (Hiking Trail), and we come to a split in the road – one going up and the other down. We keep going up, ignoring the tiny "*Wanderweg*" sign pointing down the other fork. As the road widens, we realize that this is no longer the hiking trail and retrace our steps, the real trail now mysteriously descending. As we approach the site of an old pilgrim's hostel, we know that we must be getting close, and suddenly find ourselves climbing steep steps straight up to the caves. Here the scenery is truly spectacular, and above us, yet still below the entrance to the caves, is a thundering waterfall spilling over a sharp ledge in huge sheets of water. From a nearby chapel, bells call us to prayer.

At the ticket window, we are told that we may go to the cave entrance where the cell and grave of St. Beatus are located, and stay as long as we like. To our satisfaction, we have the holy place to ourselves, except for periodic tour groups passing through to view the towering stalactites and stalagmites. The caves themselves are quite extensive.

I try to imagine someone living up here alone, and there is a helpful display to show how St. Beatus might have lived: fishing nets and drying fish hanging on a rope, fruit on the side. It seems possible. We pray at the grave (the relics were moved during the Reformation and are now in Lucerne) and at the site of his cell.

Who St. Beatus was, precisely, is a mystery, and there are several different stories associated with this name. The Beatus called the Apostle of Switzerland represents the early spread of Christianity by the apostles; exactly who exemplified this spirit in the Swiss regions – and if he was named Beatus – is too far back to know.[3]

3 See remarks about this early period in Part I, "Over the Alps".

Opposite: Pilgrim's Way to the Beatus Caves.

St. Beatus - Grabstätte
Tombe de Saint-Beat
Tomba di S. Beato
Grave of St. Beatus

IACVISSE TRADVNT CORPVS
SREGIONIS PRIMVS APOS
PERMVTAE HELVETO

It seems quite likely that there was also a holy hermit named Beatus who lived in the Beatus Caves over Lake Thun: pilgrims streamed to the spot for six centuries, there was a chapel there (destroyed in the Reformation), and a grave and parts of a skeleton were uncovered in 1903.

It is believed by some that the hermit of Lake Thun was the Irish Abbot Beatus of Honau in Alsace, whose monastery sent missionaries to Switzerland; Abbot Beatus lived in the eighth century. Another theory is that he was the founder of the monastery of Interlaken: Seliger (Beatus in Latin) of Oberhofen.

Whatever his identity, there is no doubt that his veneration by the pilgrims who came here strengthened the faith of this region. In fact, they were not even stopped during the Reformation when they were held back at swordpoint by followers of the reformer Zwingli! A stream of pilgrims mounted the cliff to his cave until the early 1900s.

We stay in the cave for almost an hour, praying and contemplating St. Beatus' life, and then sit in the little outdoor restaurant where we eat a hearty meal featuring local Swiss cheeses and "Roesti," a dish of fried potatoes. As we take the boat back to our car, the sun sets behind the mountains with streams of light piercing through the clouds, and we sit with peaceful minds and well-exercised bodies in the beauty of creation, of which God seems to have given Switzerland an abundant measure. ✢

Opposite: Grave site of St. Beatus.

ST. GALLEN: MEETING ST. GALL AND ST. OTMAR

by Pda. Margaret Bauman

St. Gallen Cathedral

In September 2012, a gathering of Russian, French, English and German speakers gathered in the old courtyard of the St. Gallen Cathedral in Switzerland. Our group included several Orthodox priests serving in Switzerland, pilgrims, and local townspeople, as well as myself (a priest's wife and American convert of German heritage) and my companion, Cornelia Delkeskamp-Hayes, a German philosopher and Orthodox convert. Cornelia had organized the tour of the cathedral, including sites usually closed to the public: the crypts of St. Gall[4] and St. Otmar (Othmar)[5], as well as a number of smaller reliquary shrines in the choir, and the St. Gall Chapel.

The Abbey of St. Gallen was built by St. Otmar in 705, on the spot where St. Gall had established his hermitage approximately a century earlier. The Abbey flourished for over 1000 years until it was secularized by local Protestant rulers in 1805, and the monks were expelled. Today the abbey buildings are still intact, and are variously used for the Roman Catholic Cathedral of St. Gall, the Abbey Library with its famous collection of old manuscripts, and other religious and governmental functions. Our purpose is to venerate the relics and honor the lives of Sts. Gall and Otmar.

4 For the *Life* of St. Gall see *Road to Emmaus*, # 41, or Maude Joynt, *The Life of St. Gall* (Llanerch Publishers, Wales, 1992).

5 St. Otmar's *Life* is not available in English, but can be read in German in *Die Lebensgeschichten der heiligen Gallus und Otmar* by Johannes Duft (Ostschweiz Druck + Verlag, St. Gallen, 1990).

Opposite: Cathedral of St. Gallen.

Saint Gall

St. Gall was born around 560-570. He probably grew up in Gaul with at least one Irish parent, and spoke Alemannian and colloquial Latin, as well as Irish.[6] He entered the monastery of Luxeuil in Burgundy as a young man, under the Irish St. Columbanus, and later became a priest-monk, serving there for at least fifteen years.

Throughout his life, St. Gall was known for his love of fishing. According to a story that St. Gall himself frequently retold, his abbot once sent him out to a certain stream to catch fish to feed guests of the monastery. Thinking he knew better, St. Gall went to a different stream, but caught nothing. St. Columbanus sent him back to the original stream – and of course now, in holy obedience, he caught ample fish.[7]

The Irish missionary St. Gall, Enlightener of Switzerland. Icon from St. Spyridon Skete.

I like to remember this story, as it demonstrates once again that sainthood and the virtues do not come full-blown, but are developed through many decisions, experiences, and struggles. And indeed, humility became St. Gall's outstanding characteristic.

Around 610 St. Columbanus lost favor with the young King Theoderic II, and was ordered to leave the country.[8] He and several other monks including St. Gall began traveling east toward Italy, but along the way were asked by the Austrasian king to stay and convert the recently-con-

6 Max Schaer, *Gallus: Der Heilige in seiner Zeit*, Schwabe Verlag, Basel, pp. 66-72.

7 George Metlake, *The Life and Writings of St. Columban*, Facsimile Reprint by J.M.F. Books, Felinfach, 1993.

8 There were apparently two issues which contributed to this: St. Columbanus' criticism of the king's promiscuity (Columbanus wanted the king to marry, but the king's grandmother Brunhilde was afraid this would diminish her power), and disagreements with the local Gallic clergy concerning the date of Easter and other matters.

Opposite: Abbey library in St. Gallen.

DEUM
INVOCO TESTEM

quered Alemanni. The monks agreed and made their first attempt in Tuggen on Lake Zürich, where St. Gall, who spoke the language, first preached to the pagans, then set fire to their temple and threw the idols into the lake. The monks barely escaped with their lives; later they would learn more effective ways of evangelizing.

At their next stop (now Bregenz, Austria) they stayed for almost two years, but because here, too, they destroyed idols, a strong faction rose up against them, and at the death of their patron, they again had to flee.

Now, St. Columbanus decided to travel on to Italy; but before their departure St. Gall became seriously ill with a fever and could not accompany him. He was nursed back to health in Arbon on Lake Constance, and then began a new phase of his life in a hermitage in the deep woods near the Steinach River waterfall (now the city of St Gallen, Switzerland) where he was eventually joined by twelve other men.

Despite his seclusion, St. Gall's holiness and the power of his prayers became known throughout the region. Implored to heal the possessed daughter of a local duke, he did so, but quickly gave away the proffered reward. He later refused both the abbotship of St. Columbanus' monastery in Gaul and consecration as bishop of Constance, preparing a local deacon named Jonathan for the office instead. Each time the result was a confirmation of the simple life he had chosen.

It seems that God's providence was at work in St. Gaul's illness, and although he had not willingly chosen to remain behind, he was able to embrace a life of humility that, from his hut in the woods (like St. Herman of Alaska), bore much fruit in true sanctity. Today, he is venerated as the Enlightener of Switzerland.

Saint Otmar

For a century after St. Gall's death, visitors to his hermitage steadily increased: hieromonks, hierodeacons, and simple monastics moved to the site to live as hermits; and increasing numbers of pilgrims came to pray, drawn by the many miracles that had occurred at St. Gall's grave. The loosely organized site was attacked more than once by robbers, until the duke on whose land the hermitages were located, invited a priest named Otmar to organize the assembly of hermitages into an ordered monastic community.

Opposite: Relics of Sts. Gall, Otmar, and other saints in the choir of the Cathedral of St. Gall, St. Gallen.

Saint Otmar (†759), whose relics are also enshrined in St. Gallen, was an Alemannian priest who restored St. Gall's hermitage a century after his death. Otmar soon attracted native Alemannian and Raetian monks and was named the first abbot of the monastery, which grew into the famous medieval Benedictine Abbey of St. Gall. Otmar also established a school, almshouse and hospital for the surrounding community, as well as Switzerland's first leprosarium, where he tended the sick. Near the end of Otmar's life, false accusations by local nobles resulted in his exile to the island of Werd in Lake Constance, but after the saint's repose his incorrupt relics and posthumous miracles testified to his holiness. Canonized in 864, his feastday is celebrated on the 19th of November.

Tour of the Cathedral

The first stop of our tour was the crypt of St. Gall under the cathedral altar, where one of the priests led us in prayer in Russian and German. We had brought along *troparia* verses from the service to St. Gall and the saints of Switzerland, and those of us who could manage the Russian tones sang the verses in German. As we venerated the relics, the Serbian priest sang a beautiful excerpt from the Slavonic *moleben* service.

After our visit to the crypt, I made a mental note that it is useful for a group to have a short talk on the saints and sites they visit beforehand, and to introduce the prayers they will use. Also, it is helpful to address the awkwardness some Orthodox Christians feel at venerating relics in a Roman Catholic church. Many Orthodox are not yet familiar with Orthodox saints of the West, nor with relics enshrined and visible within altars, as is a common European Catholic practice.

We then went up to the six small reliquary-altars lining the cathedral choir that are usually closed to the public. I was grateful to learn the dedication of each altar, and was asked by other members of the group to give some background on the lives of Sts. Gall and Otmar.

Our third site was another crypt, dedicated to St. Otmar, at the west end of the cathedral. As we progressed through the church nave, our group had begun to quiet down and now, as we stood in the silence of the crypt appreciating the closeness of the saint, the lights suddenly went out. I quietly began a hymn of praise to St. Otmar in English which Cornelia joined in, and then we repeated it in German. Just as suddenly, the lights returned and I suddenly felt very close to the saint.

Our final destination was the Chapel of St. Gall (*St. Gallus Kapelle*), which can be entered through the courtyard and marks the spot where the saint fell on his knees in the woods exclaiming, "This is it! This is where I will stay." In fact, this small chapel with the saint's relics is the most fitting place to *begin* a pilgrimage of the sacred enclosure, as it marks the original site from which the hermitage grew into the famous Abbey of St. Gall. Scenes from the life of St. Gall line the walls of the chapel, and provided a natural opportunity to explain more about his life.

St. Gall and companion fishing at waterfall of Steinach River, the site of the saint's hermitage. 1452 illustration from Codex 62, Monastery Library of St. Gallen.

When the tour finished, I went with Fr. Peter Sturm, a native Swiss priest of Russian parentage, and his Swiss Orthodox wife, to find the pond and waterfall where St. Gall had once fished. Some years before I had been thrilled to see that the pond was still full of fish like those the saint had caught; this time the pool was quiet and dark, and the fish far below the surface.

Our purpose as Orthodox pilgrims in Switzerland was to venerate saints from the period of unified Christendom and to experience the power and grace that they still pour forth in their native lands. We are grateful that the Roman Catholic Church has preserved the veneration of these saints and their relics through many difficult centuries. This was the first time our guide had seen the Eastern Christian practice of venerating relics, and told us he was moved by it. May the power of these saints bring about a renewal of Christianity in their native lands. ✢

A JOURNAL OF ORTHODOX FAITH AND CULTURE
ROAD TO EMMAUS
EMMAUS
EMMAUS
EMMAUS

WINTER 2018
ISSUE No. 72

- Orthodoxy in Greater China: Laying the Foundation for an International Orthodox Presence
- Heirs of St. Seraphim's Wonderful Revelation: The Moscow Descendants of Nikolai Motovilov
- The Motoviloffs in America: Tracking our Russian Roots
- As Bright as the Sun: Excerpts from "the Conversation of St. Seraphim and N.A. MOTOVILOV"

SUMMER/ FALL 2017
ISSUE No. 70-71

- Christianity Comes Over the Alps
- The Martyrs of the Swiss Alps
- Missionary Saints of Switzerland

WINTER/ SPRING 2017
ISSUE No. 68-69

- Pilgrimage to Lesvos: The Spiritual Treasury of a Greek Island
- Living Faith and Unsung Saints: Memories of a Holy Island
- "To Help Them Safely From the Sea…": The Heroism of Lesvos' Greek Villages
- Orthodoxy in the Urals: Remembering Verkhoturye
- Acquiring Faith: A Siberian Childhood

FALL 2016
ISSUE No. 67

- Living with Lions: The St. Mary of Egypt Animal Sanctuary
- Animals, Man and God: Orthodoxy and the Animal Kingdom
- On the Nature and Souls of Animals
- The Snakes of Markopoulo

SPRING 2016
ISSUE No. 65-66

- Saint Innocent of Alaska and Sitka's Russian-American Heritage
- Following the Star: Conversations with Sitka Elders
- Sitka's Cathedral of Archangel Michael: An Historic Russian Church in a Land of Saints
- A Russian Priest in Alta California
- Remembering Saint Innocent
- Russian Church Bells on California's El Camino Real

WINTER 2016
ISSUE No. 64

- Reflecting the Heavenly Jerusalem: Building New Churches with Dignity and Grace
- All Manner of Things Beautiful: Met. Hilarion of Kiev's Sermon on Law and Grace
- A Crown of Beauty in the Hand of the Lord: Patriarch Photios on the Restoration of Hagia Sophia

FALL 2015
ISSUE No. 63

- On Earth as it is in Heaven: Form and Meaning in Orthodox Architecture
- "Mass Transfigured By Light": The Iconic Vision of an Orthodox Church
- "We Cannot Forget That Beauty": Notes on Sources for the Conversion of Rus'

SUMMER 2015
ISSUE No. 62

- Facing Eternity in a Russian Hospice: Sustaining Compassion and Love in the Final Days
- A Peaceful Passing: Negotiating the Hospital and Hospice
- A Simple Grace
- Clothed in White Linen
- Sweet Relief: Greek Burial Rites and Ritual Lamentation

SPRING 2015
ISSUE No. 61

- On the High Road with Scotland's Saints: Six Early Christian Pilgrimage Destinations
- Columba's Children: Life and Community on a Holy Island
- How the Vikings Got Their Comeuppance: "Iona's Revenge"
- New Beginnings: Orthodoxy in Today's Scotland

WINTER 2015
ISSUE No. 60

- Chastity and Empathy: Eros, Agape, and the Mystery of the TwoFold Anointing
  An Interview in Three Parts

FALL 2014
ISSUE No. 59

- "Kicking the Earth from Under Your Feet": A Russian Scenographer on Seeing Ordinary Things in New Ways
- An Actor's Pilgrimage, A Life in Progress
- An Insatiable Desire to Share the Excitement: The Actor as a Young Man

SUMMER 2014
ISSUE No. 58

- Orthodoxy in Contemporary Sweden: From Viking-Era Christian Roots to a 21st-century Pan-Orthodox Theological Academy
- "Carrying the Tradition": Thoughts on Orthodox Parish Life in Today's Sweden
- A Swedish Princess in Kievan Rus: The Medieval Christian World of St. Anna of Novgorod

SPRING 2014
ISSUE No. 57

- A Feeling for Beauty: The Aesthetic Ground of Orthodox Ethics
- St. Theophan the Recluse: How to Love Christ
- Divine Eros in the Counsels of St. Porphyrios the New

WINTER 2014
ISSUE No. 56

- His Life in Christ: A Pilgrimage to the Holy Places of St. John of Kronstadt
- An American in Tsarist Russia: Isabel Hapgood's Meeting with St. John of Kronstadt
- In His Own Words: St. John of Kronstadt on Prayer and Warmth of Heart

FALL 2013
ISSUE No. 55

- Salvation and the Free Life of the Spirit in the Orthodox Canonical Tradition
- Nadezhda Savova's Bread Houses: Bread-Making as Food, Art, Healing, Prayer, and International Community

SUMMER 2013
ISSUE No. 54

- An Intimation of the Sacred: The Iconography of Hieromonk Silouan Justiniano
- Beauty as a Double-Edged Sword: Icons, Authenticity, and Reproductions
  I. Beyond Appearances: Classical Techniques and Sacred Painting
  II. The Iconicity of the Icon
- Incarnational Aesthetics

SPRING 2013
ISSUE No. 53

- "The Mystery that Moves the World Now Has a Name": How 150,000 Mayans Turned to Orthodoxy
- Ahora y Siempre! A Seminarian's Travels in Orthodox Guatemala
- Popol Vuh: A Mayan Tale of Creation

WINTER 2013
ISSUE No. 52

- War, Byzantium, and Military Saints
- The Opposite of War is Not Peace: Healing Trauma in *The Iliad* and in Orthodox Tradition
- Coda: Invoking God in War – Lincoln's Picture of the Second Inaugural
- Defending Russia: Belief and Coming of Age in the Soviet Army

FALL 2012
ISSUE No. 51

- Reading Hagiography: How to Engage those Astonishing, Perplexing, Archaic, and Stunningly Grace-Filled Saints' Lives
- Byzantine Bride-Shows and the Restoration of Icons: A Tale of Four Iconophile Empresses
- Early Church Writers on Hagiography

SUMMER 2012
ISSUE No. 50

- Turkey and the First Throne of Orthodoxy: A Reconsideration
- Euripides and Puccini under the Ottomans: The Surprising Richness of Greek Girls' Schools in the Late Empire
- The Seal of the Gift of the Holy Spirit: Preparing Chrism at the Ecumenical Patriarchate

SPRING 2012
ISSUE No. 49

- Natural Conception, Natural Birth: The New Hope for Infertility
- The Hospitality of Abraham: Orthodox Ethics and Reproduction
- The Embryo in Orthodox Christian Theology and Tradition
- While as Yet He Was in His Mother's Womb...

WINTER 2012
ISSUE No. 48

- Orphans in Contemporary Russia: The Russian Orphan Opportunity Fund
- Inspiration in The Making
- Orphanages and Philanthropy in Byzantium

FALL 2011
ISSUE No. 47

- A Different Light: Youthful Travelers in Contemporary America
- Death to The World: An Orthodox Punk 'Zine Revived and Revisited
- Death to The World in Print
- Catching Xenophilia: Contagious Hospitality in Orthodox Parishes

SUMMER 2011
ISSUE No. 46

- Early Orthodox in British America
- An Orthodox Christian Fired the First Shot in the American Civil War
- Louis Tikas: 1914 Passion-Bearer of the Colorado Coal Fields
- Remembering Tikas: A Pilgrimage to Loutra

SPRING 2011
ISSUE No. 45

- Croagh Patrick: The Glorious Climb of Ireland's Holy Mountain
- Asenath on the Reek
- The Spirit set in Motion: Revisiting St. Patrick's Mission to Ireland
- Over the White-Capped Sea: Eight Late Antique Irish Poems

WINTER 2011
ISSUE No. 44

- Optina's Second Spring: The Rebirth of a Russian Monastery
- Narrow Escapes of Grace: An Interview with Matusha Agapia (Minchenkova)
- The Orthodox Clock and The Map of The World

FALL 2010
ISSUE No. 43

- Taybeh's Plea For The Last Christians of The Holy Land
- The Marvellous Life of Patriarch Sophronius I, His Company of Saints, and The Fall of Byzantine Jerusalem
- The Holy City of Jerusalem

SUMMER 2010
ISSUE No. 42

- Saint Nectarios of Pentapolis: The Aegina Years
- The Great-grandmother: A Childhood on Aegina
- The Mystery of Holy Language
  - I. Liturgical Languages and Living Tadition
  - II. Coming Home to Church Greek
  - III. Defending Old Languages: Cultures, Discourse, and Heaven

SPRING 2010
ISSUE No. 41

- Coming Into One's Own Among Strangers at Home: German Orthodoxy Rekindled
- Orthodox Roots, Woods, and Water: A Decade of Pilgrimage to Germany and Switzerland
- The Advent of Orthodoxy in The German-Speaking Lands
- Pilgrimage to Eichstätt: Sts. Willibald, Walburga and Wunibald
- The Travels of Willibald: A.D. 721-727

WINTER 2010
ISSUE No. 40

- Stepping Into The Stream: An Interview with Alice C. Linsley
- Holy Wells of Wales
- The Unbroken Tradition: St. Winifred's Well (Ffynnon Wenfrewi) Holywell
- Holy Water and Pseudoscience: Who Needs Experiments on Holy Things?

FALL 2009
ISSUE No. 39

- Souls in Motion: Creativity and Community in a Harlem Workshop
- Dear Julia: Words From Souls
- Where the Cross Divides the Road (Part II)
- Babouscka: A Russian Christmas Story for Children

SUMMER 2009
ISSUE No. 38

- With The Desert Fathers of Egypt: The Coptic Church Today
- Conservation and Restoration at Sinai: Treating a Special Place Gingerly
- In The Valley There Is a Garden: The Spiritual and Cultural Treasury of St. Catherine's Monastery
- Ascent of Mount Sinai

SPRING 2009
ISSUE No. 37

- In Memoriam: Alexander Solzhenitsyn
  I. A Bright Flame II. The Homecoming III. The Turn of The Wheel
- The Orthodox Church and Society (Part II): Church-State Relations in Contemporary Russia
- The Living Relic

WINTER 2009
ISSUE No. 36

- To Be Free or Not To Be: Welsh Christianity at The Crossroads
- Safely Home to Heaven
- Melangell with a Thousand Angels
- Hare at Pennant
- The Bright Field: Three Welsh Poems
- The Orthodox Church and Society (Part 1)

FALL 2008
ISSUE No. 35

- Uusi Valamo: Finland's Northern Light
- A Short History of Finnish Orthodoxy
- Jaakko's Finland: A Village Boyhood and Beyond
- Christmas Eve: A Poem by Aleksis Kivi
- The Manifold Nature of Love The Monastery: Mr. Vig and The Nun

SUMMER 2008
ISSUE No. 34

- Greece's Dostoevsky: The Stories of Alexandros Papadiamandis
- A Village Easter: Memories of Childhood
- Mature Fruit and Bright Faith: Spiritual Direction in Contemporary Orthodoxy
- The Hidden Pearl: Rome's Catacombs and The Earliest-Known Image of The Mother of God

SPRING 2008
ISSUE No. 33

- The Life and Times of Fr. David Kirk
- Boyhood in the Deep South
- The Road to Emmaus Runs Through Harlem
- The Archbishop in Alabama

WINTER 2008
ISSUE No. 32

- The Crypto-Christians of Pontus (Part II)
- Banished Faith: The Exile of Christian Pontus
- Return To Kromni
- Between Earth and Heaven: The Monastery of Panagia Soumela
- Yuri Gagarin's Flight To The Heavens: Russia's Believing Cosmonauts

FALL 2007
ISSUE No. 31

- Faith Unseen: The Crypto-Christians of Pontus
- Confessors or Apostates?
- The Dilemma of Crypto-Christianity
- Dialogue of Civilizations: Human Rights, Moral Values, and Cultural Diversity
- The Bath House

SUMMER 2007
ISSUE No. 30

- Bede's World: Early Christianity in the British Isles
- Caedmon's Song
- Orthodoxy in Southern Italy: My Calabria
- The Land That Gave Birth to Saints
- The Children of Magna Graecia

SPRING 2007
ISSUE No. 29

- The Alaskan Orthodox Literary Resurrection
- The Angels of Akun
- Northern Climes: Father John Veniaminov's Akun Diary
- The Orthodox Worldview and C.S. Lewis (Part II)
- Notes On The Jesus Prayer

WINTER 2007
ISSUE No. 28

- The Orthodox Worldview and C. S. Lewis (Part I)
- Celtomania In Eastern Siberia
- Blessed Matrona of Moscow: Saint and Wonderworker
- Answered Prayers at St. Matrona's

FALL 2006
ISSUE No. 27

- Songs of Freedom:
- A Rastafari Road to Orthodoxy
- Nativity Address by Haile Selassie I, Emperor of Ethiopia
- 31st and Troost: From Dividing Line to Gathering Place
- Christmas in the Camp

SUMMER 2006
ISSUE No. 26

- Life on The Golden Horn: Memories of Greek Constantinople, 1948 to 1963
- Hymns and Laments on the Fall of Constantinople
- Interfaith Dialogue: An Orthodox Witness
- The Apples of Transfiguration

SPRING 2006
ISSUE No. 25

- A City of Saints:
- The Forgotten Reliquaries of Paris
- Holy France: The Pilgrim's Road
- Perspective and Grace: Painting The Likeness of Christ
- "Can These Bones Live?"

WINTER 2006
ISSUE No. 24

- Souls In Motion: The Spiritual Life of Teenagers
- Double Faith, Dostoyesvsky and Bulgakov
- Children Behind Bars: A Voice for Greece's Juvenile Offenders
- Anton Chekov: "The Student"
- The Looking Glass: Perpectives on The Teenage Years

FALL 2005
ISSUE No. 23

- Everything In Love: The Making Of A Missionary
- The Pearl of Great Price: Resurrecting Orthodoxy in China
- "I Was Born In An Orthodox World..." – Early Memories of a Chinese Christian
- The Nativity Sermon of St. John Chrysostom

SUMMER 2005
ISSUE No. 22

- Antioch's Golden Hoard: The Chalcedonian Orthodox Manuscript Treasury
- Saints and Scholars of Christian Antioch
- Pillars to Heaven: Stylite Sites of the Levant
- The Village Church of Yegorievka: Part II

SPRING 2005
ISSUE No. 21

- From Jainism to Orthodoxy: An Indian Passage
- Witness For An Apostle: Evidence of St. Thomas in India
- The Indian Verses of St. Ephrem the Syrian
- The Village Church of Yegorievka: Part I

WINTER 2005
ISSUE No. 20

- Eternal Questions: On Heaven and Hell
- The Pearl
- Christ, The Medicine of Life: The Syriac Fathers On The Lord's Descent Into Hell
- St. Milos and The Pascha Egg

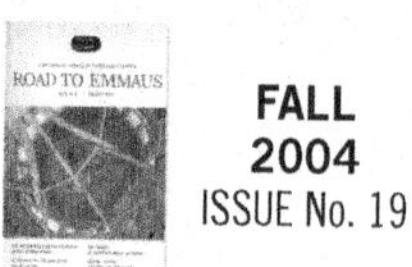

FALL 2004
ISSUE No. 19

- The Astonishing Missionary Journeys of The Apostle Andrew
- St. Andrew and The Miraculous Isle of Valaam
- Old Valaam: St. Andrew's Legacy,
- A Contemporary Photomontage
- Heaven, A Cave: Christmas in Bethlehem

SUMMER 2004
ISSUE No. 18

- We Are Going to Live in Paradise: Orthodoxy in the Congo
- Letters From An Apostle: The Inner World of Fr. Cosmas of Zaire
- The Last Priest of Caesarea
- Ascension

SPRING 2004
ISSUE No. 17

- The Golden Thread of Faith: Mental Illness and the Soul
- George, Nadezhda, Tatiana, Sergei, and Michael
- Columba Goes East
- Cadam in Ryazan

WINTER 2004
ISSUE No. 16

- Daughter of Eagles
- Albanian Diary: Ten Days in Shqiperia
- Strength in Numbers
- Orthodox Roots, Bektashi Neighbors

FALL 2003
ISSUE No. 15

- Brittany's Celtic Past
- Tro Breizh: A Pilgrimage to the Seven Saints of Brittany
- Corsican Root and Branch
- Global Perceptions and Local Relations: Pitfalls in Christian-Muslim Dialogue

SUMMER 2003
ISSUE No. 14

- Diveyevo: A Pilgrim's Chronicle
- An Album of Old Sarov and Diveyevo
- 1991: The Return of St. Seraphim's Relics to Diveyevo
- St. Seraphim's Canonization and the Russian Royal Family at Sarov

SPRING 2003
ISSUE No. 13

- Beyond the Great Wall: Orthodoxy In China
- The Lotus Cross
- The Ikon in the Home
- The Lightness of Being (Orthodox)

WINTER 2003
ISSUE No. 12

- The Bones of Contention
- Forgive Us, Merciful Lord
- Living Theology in Thessalonica
- Father Chariton

FALL 2002
ISSUE No. 11

- To Be and Not To Seem:
- My Mother-in-law, Grand Duchess Olga Alexandrovna
- 1919: A Refugee Christmas
- The Kaaba and Jacob's Pillow
- The Christmas Vigil

SUMMER 2002
ISSUE No. 10

- Embracing Spring: The Christopolous Family Of Ioannina
- Icon Of Great Joy: The Tinos Mother Of God
- Bishop Kallistos Ware On Personhood, The Philokalia, And The Jesus Prayer
- Pilgrimage Morning
- Moscow Pastors On Children, The Church, And Free Will

SPRING 2002
ISSUE No. 9

- The Stone In The Blender: Orthodox Greece And Contemporary Europe, Part II
- Saints Alive! (The Bits the Hagiographers Left Out)
- G.K. Chesterton In Russia
- Is Chesterton Worth Reading?
- Singled Out: A Survey of Orthodox Christians

WINTER 2002
ISSUE No. 8

- The Stone in the Blender: Orthodox Greece and Contemporary Europe, Part I
- The Marvelous History of the Holy Cross
- Together out of Time: Mosaics in Moscow
- A Siberian Grandmother on Confession

FALL 2001
ISSUE No. 7

- St. Nicholas Monastery and the Island of the Winds
- The Obedience of Love: An Interview with Sister Gavrilia
- Letters from a Village Matushka
- Orthodox World View: Questions from Readers

SUMMER 2001
ISSUE No. 6

- Orthodoxy in Indonesia: An Interview with Archimandrite Daniel Bambang Dwi Byantoro
- Orthodox Mission Profile: Archimandrite Daniel Byantoro and the Indonesian Mission
- The Prophet and the Pasha: Saint Cosmas of Aitolia and Ali Pasha, the Lion of Ioannina
- The Age of Wood
- Survey of Orthodox Christians

SPRING 2001
ISSUE No. 5

- My Work with English-Speaking Converts (Part III)
- From Moscow to Lindisfarne: A Pilgrimage to the West
- Contemporary Voices for Celtic Christianity
- Saints Alive! (The Bits the Hagiographers Left Out)

WINTER 2001
ISSUE No. 4

- Petersburg's Street Kids Find a Home
- Ephraim of Nea Makri: A Saint for Troubled Youth
- My Work with English-speaking Converts (Part II)

FALL 2000
ISSUE No. 3

- Russian Pickwickians: Dickens from an Orthodox Vantage
- My Work with English-Speaking Converts
- We are Once Again a People
- Christ Visits a Muzhik

SUMMER 2000
ISSUE No. 2

- Orthodox Missionary Outreach: Foma: A Magazine for Doubters
- Excerpts from Foma: So, Why is Confession Necessary?
- The House Blessing
- What Have I Done?
- The Christian Parthenon and St. Paul

SPRING 2000
ISSUE No. 1

- Fire from Heaven: Holy Saturday at the Lord's Tomb
- Teaching Our Children to Pray: Reflections of a Young Mother
- From America to Russia: The Myrrh-Streaming Icon of Tsar Nicholas II

Made in the USA
Middletown, DE
22 December 2022